I0200741

THE WAY IT WAS

Seven Days in the Heart Of Appalachia

By Matthew Wolfe

Samuel Wolfe Books
6 Maple Drive
Huntington, WV   25705

Copyright © 2017 by Matthew C. Wolfe

All rights reserved, including the right to
reproduce the book or portions thereof in
any form whatsoever, except by a reviewer
who may use brief passages for a review.

The stories in this collection are true.
Some of the details have been changed
for the sake of continuity or privacy.

Early drafts of Chapters Two, Three, and Four
were used as writing samples for which the
author received The 2005 WV Artist Fellowship
from The WV Division of Culture and History.

For additional information on Matthew Wolfe,
Visit: mysticalwolfe.weebly.com

ISBN-13: 978-0-9995196-0-8

Cover Art: Painting by William "Sarge" McGhee.
This painting of Curtis and Verna's home
was done in about 1985 for $20 and one
of Verna's home-cooked meals.
Property of Matthew C. Wolfe.

Printed in the U.S.A.

*In memory of
my grandparents,
Curtis and Verna Akers.*

ACKNOWLEDGEMENTS

It would be nearly impossible to thank everyone who contributed in one way or another to this collection that covers 45 years of my life. I won't even try.   But to all those unnamed aunts, uncles, cousins, and mountain neighbors, most of whom have passed on to the next life, I do offer my humble gratitude.

More specifically, I wish to thank my parents, Clark and Marlene Wolfe, may they rest in peace, and my Bonus Mom, Mary Sue Dameron, may she also rest in peace. Among the living relatives and friends who contributed to this story, encouraged my attempts to write it down, or made it possible for me to do the work, I must thank Dana Akers (and his delightful sisters), Deborah Allen, Anna Bailey, Bear, Ace Boggess, Brianna Bowles, David Chaffin, Nyoka Chapman, Beverly Delidow, Andrea Fekete, Sandy Farrar, Gigi Gerlach, Hayley Mitchell Haugen, Ron Houchin, Dr. Cynthia Pinson, Sharon Smith, Art Stringer, and Dwayne Walters (for whom Curtis was willing to set off his last stick of dynamite!). For giving Jeep Shiloh a second life, I must thank Dwayne Heck and Joey Heck and the mechanics at their garage: Pin

Point Auto in Barboursville, WV.

For reading early drafts of the manuscript, much thanks to The Black Dog Writers of Huntington, WV, particularly: Laura Treacy Bentley, Brenda Evans, Jen Grover, Llewellyn McKernan, Susan Maguire, Marie Manilla, Judy Freshwater Polak, Melissa Shepherd, Eileen Schley, and Diane Wellman.

On the more official side, I would like to express my gratitude to West Virginia Writers, Inc., and The Guyandotte Poets Society for their assistance.

Lastly, I am indebted to The West Virginia Division of Culture and History for the Artist Fellowship that encouraged and enabled me to complete this collection.

Table Of Contents

THE WAY IT WAS

Seven Days in the Heart
Of Appalachia

Sunday's child has open eyes,
Lives a life that's sweet and wise.
Monday's child is fair of face.
Tuesday's child is full of grace.
Wednesday's child is full of woe.
Thursday's child is has far to go.
Friday's child is kind and giving.
Saturday's child works hard for a living.

-- Nursery Rhyme

Sunday 1965

Here's a secret: Curtis wears a nightshirt when he sleeps. It looks like a shirt at the top, but comes way down to his calves.

Why do we call them calves? That's a funny word for our legs, isn't it?

Anyway Curtis wears a nightshirt like you see in the old movies and Bugs Bunny cartoons. I laugh at him when I see him wearing it, but he just smiles back at me. He was wearing it early this morning when I got up to see what the Easter Bunny left me. The Bunny left me a book, a toy car, and some candy and a stuffed rabbit with long, funny ears. The stuffed rabbit is supposed to be the one from that *Bambi* movie. You know. Thumper. So that's what I named him: Thumper. The Easter Bunny also hid all the eggs Granny and Mommy and I dyed yesterday. We dyed them red, yellow, blue, green, and purple. The kitchen smelled like vinegar, which I kinda liked. Granny says vinegar's got a "might powerful" smell, and I agree!

Curtis watched me as I hunted for all those eggs. He was wearing his nightshirt then. He's wearing regular clothes now and sitting on the front porch.

Curtis is my grandpa, but he taught me to call him "Curtis" when I was little -- I'm four now. Granny is my grandma.   They're Mommy's parents. It's hard to imagine Mommy as a little girl.

Daddy and I go out on the porch, too. Soon Daddy and Curtis are talking 'bout Curtis's new radio. It's about the size of Granny's purse, and it's covered in brown leather (Granny's purse is black and shiny). Music comes out of the radio through little holes in the leather.

Curtis says the radio has tran-sisters in it, and he likes it just fine. Daddy says tran-sister is nice, but he misses the tube radio he had in the Air Force. Curtis says he doesn't rightly know how tran-sister works, but that it's sure easy on batteries.

The man singing on the radio is Johnny Cash. He's singing something about a Ring of Fire. I'm not sure what that means, but it sounds nice.

Daddy says part of *his* name is "Cash," and

that maybe he should buy a guitar and write songs for a living. This seems strange because everyone calls him "Clark," but you never know with adults. I think Daddy is trying to be funny, but I don't get it. Curtis doesn't say anything. Sometimes I think Curtis pretends not to hear the funny things Daddy says.

I once heard Daddy tell Mommy that Curtis still doesn't think of him as "kin," whatever that means.

Anyway, I'm playing with the car the Easter Bunny left me. I'm driving it on the wicker arm of the couch we're all sitting on. I'm trying to match the tires to the strands of wicker.

Just then the weatherman comes on, and we get real quiet 'cause weather is important to grown-ups. The weatherman says it's 45 degrees out, but that it's going to warm up and be a nice, spring afternoon. When the music starts again, Curtis says that the thermometer out back is "close on to freezing," that it's always colder up here on top of the mountain.

But that's OK. Curtis's porch is enclosed with windows, and as Curtis would say, "It shore is purty" outside. I look up, and it is pretty (Mommy won't let me say "purty" or use "shore" for "sure"). There's lots of sunshine, green grass, and small, green pine trees. I can also see

Daddy's blue truck and the white picket fence. On the other side of the fence is a valley and another mountain ridge like this one. The sky is blue like Daddy's truck, and there are a couple of clouds.

Curtis has a little gas heater here on the porch to keep us warm. And he's smoking his pipe. His tobacco smoke is one of the best smells in the world.

Daddy sometimes calls these mountains "God's Country," and no one ever disagrees.

Yesterday, a man who lives "out the ridge a piece" came to visit Curtis. The man was riding a horse! Gosh, I didn't know horses were *that* big! They put me up in the saddle, and the man led the horse around a while. I held on to this thing called a saddle horn -- even though it doesn't beep or anything. It was a little scary being up that high, but it was also lots of fun.

When Daddy lifted me down, the man asked how old I was. I said four, but I wanted to say five. I'll be five in a few weeks, and that's practically grown-up.

Then the man said I did a good job. He said he figured I could be a cowboy when I get older. And that's just what I'm going to do, too. I'm going to get me a horse and come live on Akers Mountain.

But today is Sunday, which means we have to go back home.

But today is also Easter Sunday, and Granny has fixed us a big supper.

About noontime we sit down to Granny's table. Mommy has covered it with a white tablecloth. She's also put out the cloth napkins, the silver, and the fancy plates. All 'cause it's Easter. For our supper we have ham, green beans, mashed potatoes, rolls, and chocolate pie. But first, Curtis softly says a little prayer. He doesn't usually talk soft, but he does when he says the prayer.

After we eat and "rest a spell," Daddy loads our things into his truck. Then everyone else comes outside. Curtis is smoking a cigar now to help keep away the gnats. The air is good and warm, and Daddy has me and Granny and Curtis pose for lots of pictures.

After taking pictures, Mommy, Daddy, and I get into Daddy's truck, and Granny and Curtis get into Curtis's new white truck, and we all drive out the twisty dirt road a bit until we get to an old house out by the hard-top road.

Actually, the house is above an old "general store," but I don't know what that means. I just know this is where Granny Akers and Pampaw-with-the-chickens live. They're

Curtis's parents, and they're *real* old.

We all go in and take some of our Easter Supper to them. Everyone says "Hi" and "Howdy," except for Granny Akers, who doesn't get up from her chair. Mommy says Granny Akers has gone blind, which means she can't see things. Mommy leads me over to her. She's sitting next to an open window and the sunlight warms my cheeks. Granny Akers puts her fingers on my face to feel what I look like. Her hands are rough and cold. I don't like this, but I try to be good, 'cause Mommy says Granny Akers has always been special to her. And I can tell this is true by how they talk to each other.

Soon it is over, and Pampaw leads me back outside. This is one of my favorite parts about coming to the mountain: it's time to feed the chickens!

Pampaw and I go out to the chicken house. He picks up a couple of big tin cans with handles he's made out of old wire. Pampaw then fills the cans with feed from a big sack.

The chickens are already gathering around us. I guess they recognize the cans.

I dip my hand into one of the cans and grab a fistful of feed. Then I try to "fan it out" for the chickens -- only it kinda tumbles out in a clump. And here they come! Several chickens rush up to me so fast that I jump back. But I laugh too, 'cause it's funny to see them walk -- their heads goin' back and forth.

Pampaw puts some feed in a big bowl, and a lot of the chickens rush over there. I guess that's the way to do it, so I grab some more feed and put it in another bowl. But it's more fun to throw it on the ground and watch them scurry around for it, so I go back to doing that.

Mommy comes out to watch, and says, "Do you think they're getting enough food?" She laughs as she says this, so I guess she's being funny. Maybe she doesn't know how important this job is.

Pampaw answers her by saying, "I reckon they's the best fed chickens on the mountain. Maybe the county." Right then, Daddy takes another picture.

After we're done feeding the chickens, we just kind of watch them a while. I think about how we sometimes eat chickens -- maybe some of the ones I've fed before. It's kinda sad, but it makes some sense, too. Daddy and Granny have talked about killing chickens for meals -- even when they were kids, so I guess that's how it's always been.

After we leave the chickens, there's another job to do. Daddy backs his truck up to the front doors of the old store. Curtis has gotten the keys. After he opens the creaky door, we go in.

It's dark and spooky inside. It looks like the haunted houses I see in the cartoons -- only this is real! There's lots of dust and cobwebs and stuff. The windows are dirty, and the sunlight gets dirty trying to get in. There are lots of shelves everywhere. Some are stuck to the walls, and some just stand by themselves on the old wooden floor. They are all empty.

Daddy takes me behind this big counter. "Matt," he says, "Granny Akers would stand here and watch over the store." He points out at the empty space as he says this. "Over there, by the potbelly stove, men would just sit and talk and play checkers. They weren't in a big hurry.

"People would come here to visit, talk about the news, and gossip just as much as they would to shop. They'd come up here to the counter with their shopping list, and Granny Akers would get their things for them. Once the customers had everything they needed, she'd ring it up on a big cash register that sat right here." He pats the counter.

"Now," Daddy keeps talking, "Right beside the cash register, she kept her Bible, and it was always open. That way she could read it when things were slow."

"That's right," Mommy adds. She's just walked over to where me and Daddy are. "Your Granny Akers has lots of faith in God. And she read her Bible all the time. Salesmen would sometimes come and talk to her about their problems. She fed a lot of people on this mountain during the depression, when they didn't have any food. They would have gone hungry without her."

Daddy says, "Well, yes, that's right," though I can tell that wasn't something he'd planned to say. So he says, "OK, then, here was her Bible, but she was also very careful, since they lived so far away from any policemen." He points to a shelf just below the counter, "So, she kept a loaded gun right here! Under the Bible! And she knew how to use both!"

The image of the old, blind woman sitting upstairs holding a gun doesn't make much sense to me. I can't see how she'd ever have been able to run a store, let alone chase off thieves with a gun. I guess she must have been pretty tough long ago. Agin' must do bad things to you.

Then Daddy sighs, "But things are changing. We don't have many of these old country stores left anymore. Now we have grocery stores and 'Super-markets'." He says "supermarkets" like it's a bad word.

Mommy walks around for a while. Maybe she's thinking about playing in the store when she was a little girl. She's told me stories about walking on the counter when she was real little and about how folks would make over her and her curly hair.

Suddenly Mommy says, "OK, how about the metal bread shelves? We can paint those red, and Matt can keep his toys on them in the basement."

With that, Curtis and Daddy get on either side of the shelves, lift them up, and carry them out to the truck.

Mommy then walks to the end of the counter where a set of old metal shelves for packs of cigarettes is sitting. "And this," she says to me. "I can paint these blue, and you can keep small things on them, like that car the Easter Bunny left you. You like that idea?"

I smile and shake my head "yes." I didn't know we were getting things for my toys. This is a surprise. Mommy says I'm really good about takin' care of my toys, so maybe she's helping me. But I also think she wants to have a piece of the store at home.

After the truck is loaded, we're all gathered around to say good-bye -- all of us 'cept

Granny Akers. There's lots of hugs and "be sure to write" and that sort of thing.

Mommy asks Granny when they're going to finally get a telephone.

Granny says, "I reckon one of these days."

Mommy's got a tear in her eye. Daddy's getting that look he has when he's been at work all day. I guess, like me, they really don't want to leave the mountain.

I look up and see Granny Akers sitting by her window. She looks lonely. I feel sad. I want to do something for her. Suddenly I remember something new in Daddy's truck. I go over and open the door. Then I reach in and pull out my new, shiny little brief case. Aunt Mary sent it to me all the way from Florida. She says I can use it this fall when I start kindergarten. Right now I have lots of toys in it. I turn around and hold it up high.

"Look, Granny Akers! I have a briefcase for when I go to school."

Then I remember: she can't see me or the briefcase. I'm not even sure if she can hear me. But she looks even sadder now, like everything is comin' to an end.

Maybe she misses the store.

Maybe it has something to do with

change.

I hear that word a lot: "change."

Maybe it has to do with change and tran-sister.

Or maybe she did hear me and doesn't like briefcases.

Then I remember, cowboys don't carry briefcases. I bet she knows that and is sad for me.

Mommy calls up to her, "Bye, Granny. We love you." Granny Akers smiles, just a little, and waves down toward us.

Then Mommy, Daddy and I get in the truck. I sit in the middle. I love this truck. Daddy says maybe he'll get seatbelts for it -- whatever that is.

As soon as we pull out onto the hardtop road, Mommy starts cryin'. She says she doesn't think Granny Akers will live much longer. I'm not sure what this means. I wonder if it is anything like going blind.

I snuggle up against Mommy, clutching Thumper in my arms.

Mommy puts an arm around me as we drive the long winding road off the mountain, and I go to sleep.

"Great Granny Akers"
Cozettie Ann Cook Akers
September 19, 1886 –
        February 24, 1966

"Pampaw With the Chickens"
James Riley Akers
August 2, 1881 –
        April 8, 1970

Monday - 1972

I wake up to the smell of a fresh mountain breeze blowing up from the valley and in through my window; it's a cool August morning. Back home it's already in the 90s, but this week, I'm at my grandparents' house up on the mountain. I'm eleven years old, and for the past couple of summers I have spent a week living with Granny and Curtis.

I get up, dress in my play clothes, and head out into the kitchen. It's not yet eight o'clock, but Granny has already done a day's work: cooked breakfast, made Curtis' lunch, made their bed, done the morning dishes, and pulled out her pressure cooker and a couple of dozen glass jars for canning. Right now she's sitting at the kitchen table, wearing a clean summer dress with a plaid print that I particularly like. She made that dress herself. Granny has hair that has mostly turned gray by now, and she has been stringing green beans for over an hour. She looks like what you'd expect a grandma to look like.

Today is a canning day. By mid-afternoon, she'll have put up about two-dozen cans of beans, and there'll be more over the next few days.

Granny looks up at me and smiles; her smiles are infectious, full of energy and spunk, and, if you look closely, you'll even see mischievousness darting about in her eyes. I can tell she's amused by my messy morning appearance. She and I have a very strong bond now. Just four months ago I was a fairly sick kid in the hospital. The nurses were insensitive, whiny, and lazy. Granny took over and gave orders.

After I left the hospital, she stayed with my parents and me to help at home for a week. In addition to helping with the meals, laundry, and caring for me, she also found plenty of time to beat me at Chinese checkers several times each day.

Now we're smiling at each other in a goofy-morning sort of way.

"How are you this mornin'," she asks.

"Fine," I say as I head to the bathroom to wash up.

When I return to the kitchen, she pulls a plate from the oven. She's been keeping bacon and fresh biscuits warm for me. I normally don't like to eat breakfast, but I do when I am with my grandparents. "This good mountain air sure makes a little fella hungry," she says with a laugh.

After breakfast, I head outside to soak up more of the air and the sun. My "playground" is the soft grass and trees that surround a modest white and green trimmed house, built on the top of a mountain some people call "Akers Mountain." The house sits on the mountain ridge and is nestled next to a hillside. There are two gardens (the upper and the lower) on opposite sides of the house, a couple of small tool sheds, a homemade camper that Granny and Curtis lived out of when they drove to Alaska four years ago, a white picket fence, gravel driveway with lush green grass running down the center, pine trees, a picnic table, an outdoor fireplace, and a swing.

I think I'm now too old to play the imaginary games of war and cowboys and Indians that I played just a summer ago. But I find plenty to do: climbing on the fence, climbing trees, and studying dew covered spider webs in the many flowerbeds. There are no kids living on this mountain (not many people, period), but I'm never bored. I know most of my friends would be, but somehow I fit perfectly into this life and never have trouble finding something to do.

By late morning, I'm shooting a basketball. Curtis recently put this hoop up on one on the sheds, and yesterday Granny came out and shot a few baskets with me. I hate to admit it, but she's as good as I am. She tells me she played on the girls' basketball team in high school. She was tall, still is, and proud of it. Me? I'm a little – ok, a lot, behind the other boys in school.

Suddenly I hear Granny yelling for me, "Hey, Squirt! ("Squirt" is her pet name for me, and I love it); it's time for dinner (lunch)." She'll try to get me to eat fried bologna again, but I'll probably have a chicken leg left over from last night's supper (dinner). That and a big piece of chocolate pie (she has a secret recipe, you know).

Soon, I'm back outside and full of pie. I stretch out on the big swing under the pines and a lonely maple. For a long time, I just swing back and forth, watching the blue sky and the clouds. There's a gentle breeze that rustles in the pines and the huge willow tree behind me. It's so quiet and soft out like this.

I must have fallen asleep, 'cause the sound of a car on the gravel road just beyond the fence wakes me up. It's the mailman in his little car. It's the first car to go by in hours; I guess that's why it woke me up. I get up and walk across the road in my bare feet to get the mail. The little stones don't hurt anymore. After three months of summer, my soles are pretty tough. On my way up the path to the backdoor of the house, I realize that there are hundreds of grasshoppers hopping in the grass. They're everywhere! And I have a great new idea.

Rushing into the kitchen and handing her the mail, I blurt out, "Granny, can I have a jar and lid?"

"Whatever for?" She asks as she looks through the letters.

"To catch grasshoppers. Curtis said he'd take me fishing tomorrow, and they'll make great bait."

Granny goes over to the basement steps, opens the door, and reaches up to a shelf for a big, empty peanut butter jar and lid. She hands them to me.

"Go downstairs and use a nail to poke some holes in that lid. You'll want those hoppers to still be hopping tomorrow," she says as she flips through the mail.

I head for the stairs, but she stops me.

"Hold on there, now. Ya got a letter from your folks; don't you want to read it?"

I grab the letter from her hands, head down the steps, and say, "I'll read it outside."

The basement/garage is a magical place. Cool and dark, it has a coal bin and a coal furnace, a wood stove, a ringer washer, and lots of tools. Curtis is a mechanic, and he has his garage pretty much outfitted for work on his truck, the lawn mower, and the rotor-tiller. The basement has a smell that's an incredible blend of grease, coal, detergent, earth, wood, and, of course, mountain air from an open window. I set the jar and letter on the small, worn workbench, lift the hammer from its place on the wall, and begin to look for the right-sized nails.

Dozens of glass jars hang down from the ceiling. Curtis nails the metal lids of these jars to the joists, fills the jars with bolts, nuts, screws, washers, nails, and everything else small enough for a jar. Also hanging from the ceiling are fishing rods, a miner's lantern, pieces of scrip, Styrofoam ice chests, and the shotgun.

Last year I was afraid to come down here by myself, but this year I'm grown up.

I finally find the right nails, unscrew the jar from its lid, and carry it to the bench. I grab a nail, whack a few holes in the metal lid, and return the nail jar to its place on the ceiling. And, after hanging the hammer back up in its proper place, I open the garage doors, big carriage style doors that swing out to either side.

In a matter of minutes I have a jar full of grasshoppers. Tomorrow will be a good day to fish, and we'll have fresh trout and bluegill for supper. I like it that I now know how to clean my own fish. It feels good to be able to catch your own meals.

With my jar full, I sit down under the willow tree, pull the letter from Mom and Dad out of my pocket and read it. They complain about the heat back in Huntington and fake jealousy that I'm up where it's so cool and no one has or needs air conditioners. There's also a few cartoons they clipped from the newspaper, things which reminded them of me.

About that time, Granny calls me in to take a bath and get ready for supper.

When I get out of the shower, I find out Curtis has just gotten home, so I rush in to see him. I immediately grab his dinner pail (lunch box) and fling it open. Inside, I find a Hershey Chocolate Bar. He puts his big hand on my head and rubs my wet hair and laughs. "Matchew," he says, playing with my name, "what'd you do today?"

"I got some grasshoppers for our fishing trip."

He just laughs some more and heads in for his shower. I know he'll spend a long time trying to scrub the grease out from under his fingernails, 'cause we're going to a wake after supper.

I take the candy bar to my room. I know better than to ask if I can eat it now, this close to supper. I also know that Granny puts these daily candy bars in the dinner pail when she packs it in the mornings -- they don't know I know, and I sure don't want to tell them. It might put an end to these daily treats; besides, I think we all have fun with the game.

But things are kind of different at supper tonight.

Usually there's lots of talk about the gardens, the weather, family, fishing trips, and even world affairs. But tonight, we all seem a little quieter. It's strange, 'cause we're all dressed up for the wake. Granny is particularly nice looking; she is, as always, a lady. Graceful, neat, and smart, I guess she doesn't fit the stereotype of mountain folk. But there it is;

neither of them do. Curtis actually watches opera on public TV! Of course, that's when "professional" wrestling isn't on. I am aware of the complexity of people, and it fascinates me no end.

Granny finally talks about it: "How old was she, Curtis?"

"John said she just turned four a few weeks ago."

"That's a shame," Granny says, taking a sip of her coffee.

"Shore is."

It takes us about 45 minutes to drive to the funeral home. That's how far it is from the mountaintop to the closest town of any real size.

I had never seen a child's casket before, didn't know there was such a thing. Inside is a pretty little girl, the daughter of one of the men Curtis works with. She has on a frilly pink dress and holds a doll. Her blonde hair matches the doll's. Until now, all the viewings I had been to were for old people.

This is something very different. It floors me. I join Curtis and all the other men out in the foyer where there are benches.

An old man is telling a story. Every once in a while he makes big motions with his hands in order to tell the story better. He's missing the better part of three fingers on his right hand. Every time I come to a funeral or wake in the mountains, including those for Granny Akers and Pampaw, I see these old men with lots of missing parts. Fingers, hands, sometimes legs. Dad once told me that these old guys often lost fingers working in the coalmines or in the sawmills making props for the mines. These men worked in the mines long before there was a union to improve working conditions. So I sit here watching this guy tell a story with his thumb and index finger. But my mind keeps shuffling back and forth from wondering how this man lost his fingers to the image of the little girl in the room behind me.

Later, on our way home, I ask, "Granny, why would God let a little girl die?"

"Well, Matt, I don't rightly know, but God has a purpose for everything, so we just leave it in his hands."

Now, I had already heard that answer from other adults a dozen times before, but when Granny said it there was no doubt but what she truly believed that. It made all the difference in my mind. I knew it to be true.

After we get home, Curtis and I watch a little TV, and I eat my candy bar. We are all very quiet. The sun is setting and the entire mountain seems to slip into a restless dream. When I lay down in bed, I remember what Granny has said, and realize that each of us has a purpose to fill in life. I wonder for a while about what mine might be. Then my mind drifts to fishing, and I fall into a deep sleep.

Tuesday, 1976

I'm awakened by a commotion out in the kitchen. Granny is on the phone, and she is very angry. I have only heard her this angry once before. It is a rare tone of voice. I quickly pull on my old clothes and stagger out to the kitchen. I'm worried that there is something terribly wrong. I'm 15 years old now, and I'm aware of how fragile my grandparents' health has become. A couple of days ago Curtis had several skin cancers removed, and we've all become aware of the fact that his lungs are black from all the coal dust he was been exposed to during his years working in and around the mines. Granny, too, has started showing little signs of aging; high blood pressure and thyroid medicine are part of her daily regime now. Yelling on the phone can't be a good thing.

Granny looks up at me standing in the door and half waves as she continues her attack.

"Now, Shelby, I don't care if you *do* have to skip your breakfast. You come on down here and get this cow outta my garden right now! She's eatin' my corn and trampling my tomatoes. Are you listening to me? I mean now!"

Apparently the neighbor's cow has managed to get through the fence and is inflicting great injuries on Granny's garden. I find the whole thing amusing, but keep my smile hidden. Granny's garden is off limits to jokes.

After hanging up on Shelby, Granny looks at me. She blinks her eyes, nods her head once, and says "Wow!" all at the same time. It's a wonderful habit she has that lets us all know she's riled up, feisty, and ready to take on the world single-handedly. "Well, I reckon I better get back," she says, "and see what that ol' cow has left me." And just like that she's back out the door headed for her garden.

Looking over at the kitchen table, I see Curtis sitting there with a big smile on his face. "Your grandmother shore does like her garden," he says.

I smile back and say, "Yeah, she does." Then I pull a plate of hot biscuits and sausages out of the warm oven and sit down across from him.

Curtis is retired now, but they still get up early as ever. He's having a coffee break and is ready for a cigarette. He pulls a pouch of tobacco and a book of rolling papers out of his shirt pocket and begins filling and rolling his own.

"Of course," he says as he licks the edges of the paper, "Verna actually did shoot a cow once."

"What?!"

"She sure did. She was about your age, and one day she found a cow in her garden and went back an' got a rifle outta the house. She was aiming to miss, to shoot over the cow's back an' just scare it good. But she shot it instead."

He stops to light his homemade cigarette with a wooden match. To be specific, it is a Diamond brand match. "Strike on the Box." The Red, White, and Blue box. The sound of the match as he strikes it against the emery cloth on the side of the box is magical to me. A second later the wonderful smell of the match reaches me. It is a comforting smell that reminds me of camping and Curtis and all that seems good in life. Then I smell the smoke from his cigarette. I love that smell, always will. It's a clean, earthy smell of fresh tobacco that no factory cigarette can offer.

With the ritual of lighting the cigarette out of the way, I ask, "Did Granny kill it?"

"Oh, no. Didn't even hurt it much. The bullet went clean through her belly."

I'm a little disappointed that the cow lived, but it's still pretty cool to think that your grandmother shot a cow just because it was standing in her green beans.

After breakfast, I head outside to paint some more of the white picket fence. This isn't the fence the wayward cow waltzed through. That's a wire fence along the upper garden. The picket fence is more of a decorative fence along the road in front of the house (though it does help stop the snow from drifting in the winter). This fence is somewhat the pride of the mountain. It is actually mentioned as a landmark when folks are trying to give directions to their homes out in these parts. I have been scraping and painting on it for several days now. If I get busy, I can probably finish it today.

For a while I think of myself as a Tom Sawyer of sorts, but it really doesn't wash. For one thing, I actually enjoy this work. I like painting. I like being outside in the mountain air and under the peaceful pine trees, and I like doing something that helps my grandparents --

Oh, and they'll pay me for the work, too. It so happens I've had my eye on an electric guitar at the music store.

Soon I've fallen into a rhythm of painting and feel very good as the sun bakes my back. I've also been counting the cars that pass me on the road: four. It's a busy day.

And before I know it, Granny is calling me in for dinner. We're all three hungry and dig into our home-made egg-salad sandwiches without much talking.

Soon, Granny is up and ready to head out to the garden again. She mutters something about picking a mess of beans for supper. Curtis and I lean back to digest and listen to the news on his radio. Curtis makes another cigarette. But before long Granny is back, madder than a hornet. She heads straight for the phone.

"Shelby, that cow is back in my garden!" She shouts into the receiver. "Well, I don't care what you have to do. You come down here, get this cow, and get your boys to fix that fence."

Curtis and I are looking at each other smiling. After all, my grandparents are not destitute. Elsie-the-cow could level the whole garden -- both gardens even, and they wouldn't go hungry. Money is not the issue here. It's just funny to see Granny so riled up about something.

Finally, she hangs up abruptly and leaves through the basement door. This is rather odd, because she's working in the upper garden and her tools are already out. There's no reason to go through the basement and out the garage doors. Curtis and I look at each other, puzzled. I think it hits us at the same time. The shotgun is in the basement.

I'm hot on Curtis' heels as we rush down the basement steps. He can still move faster than I give him credit for.

When we get to the basement floor, I peer over his shoulder, and sure enough, Granny is headed out the garage door, the shotgun in her hands. Something tells me she isn't going to aim to miss this time. I cannot believe she is this upset about a few ears of corn.

Curtis catches up with her in the front yard. He stops her by gently placing his hand on her arm. She turns, and they look at each other for a moment. Finally, without any discussion, she hands him the gun. It's a touching scene. She's not surrendering the gun. He hasn't given her a dirty look to get her to turn it over. It's just that his presence at her side has reminded Granny that this isn't the right thing to do. The love they share is genuine, and their years together make words unnecessary. Granny

32

smiles a little bit and returns to her garden, empty handed.

I head back to the pickets, and in less time than you might expect, Shelby's boys have rounded up the cow and mended the wire fence.

About an hour later, Curtis comes out of the garage with a big broom and yelling, "Bear, Hey Bear!" His voice echoes off the ridges, and I wonder what someone just visiting would think. They'd probably look around in fear and wonder why he's carrying a broom of all things -- *now* would seem like the time for the shotgun.

Curtis yells again. "Bear! Where are you? Heeeeeyyyy Bear!"

It isn't long before a large, black German shepherd comes running from over the hillside and across the road.

I'd like to say that the nearest house to Granny and Curtis is 12 miles "yonder." But that's not the case. Curtis built a little cottage about 100 yards from his house and rents it out to the Johnston family, Verlin and Ellen, and their son, John. Bear is their dog.

Bear rushes past me without a glance and runs right up to Curtis. The dog leaps at Curtis, and I am always afraid he'll get knocked down. In point of fact, Bear has knocked me down a couple of playful times -- but he seems to know not to be so rough with Curtis.

"Now settle down, Bear," Curtis says through his own laughter. "That's right. Now, Bear, lay down there. Bear, I don't want no trouble."

Finally Bear lies down in the soft grass and Curtis begins sweeping the dog with the broom. It's grooming time, a joy they share just about every day the weather permits.

By mid-afternoon, I am closing in on the painting job. If I really go after it, I can finish by supper, but Curtis has a different idea. He wants to go for a drive of all things. I start to protest, because this means I'll have to finish this last section tomorrow. I want to whip out one of those country expressions about "Why put off tomorrow" and all, but I know it won't play here. Besides, when do you ever hear these old country folk actually use those expressions? I never once heard Granny say, "A bird in the hand . . ." or "A stitch in time . . ." or any other of those quaint expressions that the "experts" in my West Virginia History book told me all mountain folk use. She did tell me once that if the sun shines while it's raining, it's a "sure sign the devil is beating his wife."

But Curtis wants to go for a drive, so I

wash out my brushes and climb into his car.

We drive out to the highway, cross it, and follow the dirt road out the mountain ridge to the west. Curtis is driving, of course; I still don't have my learner's permit, but I hope against hope that he'll let me drive anyway. It's not like you're going to run into anything resembling law enforcement out here, and the farther we go, the more remote the world gets. We take one turn-off after another, and pretty soon, I'm lost. Curtis loves to play with my sense of direction. After awhile he'll say, "Matt, I think we're lost." And he'll try to get me to prompt him on the way to get back home. It scared me a little when I was a kid, but now I realize this game improves my sense of direction.

After what seems like an eternity, we pull down into a little, scenic valley. There is a small weathered house and a large garden. Out in the garden is a little old man hoeing his beans in the hot sun. Curtis pulls into the drive, and the man immediately drops his hoe and walks up to the car. He says, "Well howdy, Curtis," and leads us into his humble home.

The man is even older than I first thought, and it is soon obvious that he lives alone. His tiny house is sparsely outfitted and neat, everything in its place, but it could stand a good cleaning. Still, it is a cool and friendly place to be. The windows are open (without screens), and a gentle breeze blows through with the fresh fragrance of summer on it. We all sit around a rickety kitchen table.

Curtis introduces me as kin: "This is Marlene's boy."

Then the two men forget all about me and begin talking. The trouble is, I have no idea what they are talking about. The little old man has a dialect so thick, I cannot understand him. What's more, Curtis slips into an almost identical dialect, just like shifting gears in a comfortable old car. For about thirty minutes, I sit quietly listening to a language I do not know. At first I am a bit irritated; I feel left out. But I quickly get over that and just let my mind drift. That's when I begin studying the house. A couple of shotguns hang on the wall; they are well cared for. A "mess of beans" lies on a towel by the sink. And the sink is manned by an old, hand-operated water pump. Duct tape holds a handle onto one of the pots. There is an obvious absence of anything recently bought at any store. No cans of food or bottles of pop or boxes of cereal. Nor are there any cabinets to hold these things. Curtis has brought me to see a real mountain man, a man who, for the most part, is self sufficient and independent. This hermit probably has no bank account. I don't see a phone or TV, and, while he has electricity, the proximity of his kerosene lamp to his wood stove leads me to believe he'd be just fine without the power company.

Suddenly I want to understand what this man is saying. I try, but all I can pick up is that he only goes to Matoaka a couple of times a year now. The crowds are awful (Matoaka's population is about 1000). And there is no way he is ever going back to Princeton (population 7000) -- a man could get in trouble there. Mountain Man talks about his 'seng -- ginseng he collected in the woods and sold for about $40 a pound dried. And he talks about his garden and how he'll put up enough food to last him the winter. He still hunts (though I doubt he has a hunting license -- heck, I doubt he has a Social Security card). And that is about all of the conversation I can get, but it is enough. I realize that sitting in front of me is a true mountain hermit who lives off the land and who needs no help from anyone else, thank you. This is a man who has his feet firmly planted in another life, another age. And he is a dying breed.

I also realize that Curtis has a foot in that world as well. If push comes to shove, if the structure our modern world is built upon collapses, Curtis would survive. So would Granny, and the many other people who live in these mountains. They have the spirit of adventure and work and making the best with what nature, that is, God, provides. And staring at this little old man and my grandfather, I am suddenly in awe of them. I wonder if I have that spirit as well.

For supper, Granny serves corn on the cob, green beans, and potatoes -- all from her garden. We also have hamburgers; the meat came from her brother's cattle farm. She and Curtis helped dress and prepare this meat. Curtis slices a fresh tomato for his burger, a tomato he plucked from a plant just outside the back door about ten minutes ago. Granny made the pickles. Only the buns, mustard, and ketchup came from a store.

It wasn't that many years ago that Granny kept chickens, a cow, and a horse. In fact, when she and Curtis first married, the Great Depression had just started. Part of their livelihood came from the eggs, milk, and butter she sold from horseback. Yeah, these are tough people.

I look around the kitchen -- just to

compare it with Mountain Man's. There isn't much comparison. My grandmother has a nice, modern kitchen. But look closer. A kerosene lamp sits on top of a cabinet. In the basement is a wood burning stove as well as the wood and coal furnace. In fact, just below my feet is a cistern with hundreds of gallons of water. It dawns on me that while Curtis worked hard to buy a few modern conveniences, they are still self-sufficient in a way most of America can only imagine.

If Granny's reaction to a cow in her garden seemed overboard this morning, not anymore. She was protecting their independence, their food store, their very way of life.

After supper, we head outside to the fireplace. Even in early August, the evenings are so cool that you need to light a fire to sit outside and relax.

Looking into the glowing embers, I come to the conclusion that I do have that independent spirit. It may not be so obvious, and I know that I am more dependent on the modern world than I would care to admit, but the spirit is here. And I realize, too, that it came from my pilgrimages to this mountain; this spirit is being passed to me by my grandparents. It is contagious after all.

Wednesday, 1982

I wake up to the sound of rain on the tin roof over my head. The splatter, patter, and muffled-pings of drops striking metal creates a never-ending and random rhythm. It is a music with a natural sense of time rather than a measured cadence constructed by human cleverness. It's a wonderful sound. I could sleep forever under such a sound.

The rain is also good, because we need to refill the cistern. It's been a dry summer. But I worry about the rain as well. Acid from factories and power plants that belch coal smoke is mixing with the precipitation and polluting the water we drink. Studies show that the acid has been quite prevalent here in southern West Virginia.

The outside world is invading life on the mountain. I am 21, and want to save the world, but have no idea how. I've become an angry young man. But here, at this special home on the mountain, the anger disappears.

After a leisurely time gazing out the window at the lush green valley, I pull myself out of my cocoon, dress, and head out to the kitchen.

Curtis is enjoying his mid-morning coffee and a doughnut. I get some bacon out of the oven and grab a doughnut as I sit down next to him. I'm pretty groggy, so after our "Good mornings," we just sit there in silence.

After a little while, I feel the trickle of hot fluid on the back of my hand. Without looking, I know what has happened. Curtis has dribbled a little of his hot - though not scalding - coffee from a spoon and onto the back of my hand. It's a game he's been playing for as long as I can remember.

I make a fake angry face and turn toward him.

"Now Matt! I don't want no trouble." He says this with a big smile on his face. He puts his hands up and open between us as if he really expects me to take a swing at him -- an impossible idea.

I just laugh a little and go back to my

bacon.

After another spell he says, "If it's OK with you, I thought we'd drive over to the bridge today. I reckon it'll quit raining by noon, at least for a bit."

He means the big bridge over the New River. It is quite a sight.

"Sure." I reply, and he goes off to shave. I think about reminding him that just last night the weatherman said it'd rain all day, but decide it doesn't matter.

After I finish eating, I go up to the attic to visit Granny. Obviously she can't work in the garden today, what with the rain and all. This attic space is more of a half-story room, the ceiling slants down in angles that trace the bottoms of the roof's rafters. It is a little under six-feet high at the center, and I can no longer stand up straight.

I find Granny sitting at her quilting frames threading a needle. These are old, oak frames that she has used for decades to make dozens of quilts. Many of them have been quilts she's pieced together -- patchwork quilts -- warm, beautiful quilts made from bits of this and that. Even now, I see a piece of the plaid fabric she used to make a dress from when I was a kid. And there's a piece of one of the shirts I outgrew before it got any wear. There's a lot of history in one of these quilts, even before it's finished.

Beyond the frames is a nice-sized pair of windows that were installed, side-by-side, when Curtis built this house back during the depression. It amazes me that he did most of the work himself.

There are also some beans hanging from the ceiling to dry, and some boxes of things that have been stowed here. This "attic" is as clean and practical and neat as the rest of the house, and it is a fun place to be on a cool, damp summer day.

There's even an old trunk stuck up here. It was put up here before the frames for the door were finished, and they're not sure if they can ever get it out.

Not that it matters; Granny and Curtis think they will live here forever.

I try to absorb this moment. I intentionally try to remember everything. It's a habit I've developed. I know this will all end eventually. They will die someday, and I dread it terribly.

I've also become aware of the fragility of their very lifestyle, the lifestyle of all mountain people. It's more than the acid rain. McDonald's and discount stores and Coke and the rest are going to take all this away. Corporate America is seeping into everything and destroying independent spirits. And I wonder if there is any way my life can be as poetic as that of my grandparents when I reach their age. I seriously doubt it, but I vow to try.

With all this in mind, I pull up a chair, sit down close to Granny, and watch her work the needle through the top, the cotton, and the backing. Slowly she makes graceful arcs that fan out across the fabric and hold everything securely in place. As she does this, she tells me stories about my mother as a little girl ("the prettiest little girl on the mountain, with her Shirley Temple dresses and curly blonde hair"), about the trip to Alaska to be there when my cousin Anna was born ("first time I ever flew on a plane, don't you know"), and stories about dating Curtis. I've heard them all a dozen times or more, but it always feels like the first time. And then, she tells me about how much she loved to dance the Charleston. This is something new, and I stare at this beautiful woman and try to imagine her as a Flapper, dancing in the roaring 20s. I realize at that very moment, if I could board a time machine and go back to see anything in history, I would choose to see my seventeen-year-old grandmother dancing the

Charleston. I promise myself to find some old music and have her show me how to dance -- someday.

After an early lunch, Curtis and I drive to the bridge. I'm driving, of course. He leaves the driving to me these days so he can look around and play navigator.

And he was right. It has stopped raining.

When we reach the bridge, we pull off at the overlook. The New River Gorge Bridge is the longest single span bridge in the world: 1700 feet, and the second highest in the United States: 876 feet. The gorge is a breathtaking sight, a wild and rugged valley carved out by one of the world's oldest rivers. The sweeping arch of the bridge, the brown steel nestled among the pine trees, seems to accent the beauty of the gorge -- not destroy it. It reminds me of photographs I've seen of Frank Lloyd Wright houses. Man can build in nature without utterly destroying it. These things are possible.

Curtis comments on the men who died or were injured building the bridge, on the men who have died building so many of the things we use in this world. Each day thousands of people drive across this bridge without thinking about the sacrifice, the labor, the blood. Curtis has a knack for turning the ordinary into something sacred.

Then, a hawk soars over the gorge, and my thoughts return to the beauty of this place.

A couple of hours and two milkshakes later (Curtis never misses the chance for a good milkshake), we're almost home. It's raining again, pouring, as Curtis predicted.

Just after we pull off the main highway and turn toward his house, Curtis asks me to pull off the road

"Matt, I think we'll just sit here and wait out this rain. You ain't in any hurry are ya?"

"Nope," I reply.

I shut off the engine and listen to the rain on the top of the car. It's not as nice as the tin roof, but it'll do. Curtis makes a cigarette -- slowly, patiently -- and strikes the wood match. We sit quietly and watch the rain, lost in our own thoughts.

We are parked near the site of Curtis' parents' old home. This is where Great Granny Akers and Pampaw-with-the-chickens had the general store. The house and store burned down a few years ago, and the chicken house and other buildings settled in on themselves long before that. One of my cousins owns this land now, but he hasn't "seen fit to do nothin' with it." And right now I think that's for the best.

There was a small porch not 25 feet from where we're sitting now, and I can remember a little bit about sitting on that porch. I can remember the slow pace of life, the rhythm of it all, the cousins and uncles who played with me there one fine summer day.

I look over at Curtis, and realize that his memories of this place go back 50 years beyond my own. I can remember the many, many stories he's told me about this mountain. And he is sitting here waiting for the rain to let up, to savor this place, this land -- to enjoy the moment.

Curtis can be impatient at times, but for the most part this is his nature. When he sees someone driving too fast or passing in a dangerous place, he'll say, "They's in a hurry" or "He's in an awful hurry." These are calm announcements, as if he wonders just why people are always in such a rush, maybe even questioning times that he, too, gets in a hurry. And from what I've heard about his father and from what little I remember, I sense that Pampaw-with-the-chickens was about the same -- wondering where everyone's going in such a hurry.

For the second time today, I try to absorb this moment, this time. I try to savor it and learn the same lessons. And I wonder if there is any way I can possibly show the same patience and pace in a world that is growing faster with each passing day.

Curtis breaks the silence: "Matt, you ought to tow that pick-up truck up here sometime. We can work on it together and get it going again."

Curtis means the blue '53 Ford truck, the same one I remember sitting in a few yards from here, where he and Dad loaded the shelves from the store. Dad kept it, though it hasn't run in years. We keep saying we'll get around to restoring it -- someday. This is not the first time Curtis has suggested we work on it together.

All I can think to say is, "That'd be nice, Curtis. Real nice."

But restoring it in Curtis' garage would take more than the week I usually spend up here each summer. Probably all summer and more. And Curtis, the retired mechanic, knows that, too. Sometimes I wonder if he is suggesting, subtly, that I come live with them for a while. It is a thought I have considered myself. It is daring to ponder.

I *am* still in college, working toward a career in music. And even though graduation with my bachelor's degree is still a year away, professor A wants me to get a master's degree in music performance. Professor B says it should be in musicology, and everyone else seems to think I should get an MA in *something*. Deep down I suppose they are right.

I also have a girlfriend/fiancé-in-waiting, Kim, who doesn't yet understand my need for music or the mountain. But she will -- someday.

And I have an idea. Next year, I will make a summer-long stay here. I'll bring up the truck, and Granny will teach me how to dance the Charleston. It'll be great. And if, for some reason, I can't, then the following summer -- there's still time.

But for now, the rain has let up, and Curtis has finished his cigarette. I start up the car, and we head for home.

After supper and the news, Granny, Curtis, and I go out to the enclosed front porch. It's chilly, so Curtis lights the gas heater and smokes his pipe. Granny writes in her diary. We sit in luxuriant silence. The rain has finally stopped for good, and a fog is rolling in around the picket fence. I realize that it will need painting again next summer, but that's all right. I have a plan.

After a while, Granny goes to bed and

Curtis soon follows.

I sit alone and meditate on nothing in particular. Silence like this brings on moments of clarity. For the first time, I realize just how special this place really is. On the mountaintop beside of the house is a point where Dad and I flew a kite when I was quite young. The sun and the wind that warm spring day filled me with the same inner peace I feel now. Then there are the countless times that I have felt this peace by the fire behind the house or on this porch.

And it occurs to me that I only feel this way when I am out in nature or when I am playing music, and what is music but a form of nature?

The stresses and pressures that come from words like "Career" and "Future", and "Commercialism" melt away with melodies from instruments or babbling brooks. "Getting Ahead," "Goals," and "Healthy Income" scatter when the wind whistles through the pines.

Curtis often says I work too hard. I used to think he was kidding, but now I'm not so sure.

If I bring the old truck up here to restore, and if we go for rides to look for parts, visit with old mountain men, and stop for milkshakes, it might take us well over a year to "finish the job," to "reach the goal." And a part of me wants that, desperately.

But another part of me has dreams and schemes. Is there anyway to balance these? I want to believe there is -- but underneath my denial, I know better.

This confusion of heart and mind has me restless now. So I do what's best for such feelings. I go to my room and retrieve the folk guitar I brought up to the mountain with me. It's actually Dad's guitar. He got it when I was about eight or nine, but he was never able to do much with it. I assumed ownership. I've named it "Becky."

I come back out to porch, close the door behind me, and softly strum and pick a series of riffs and tunes and chords. I play nothing in particular.

I play in the glow of the gas stove. I look out on the yard and the fence and the fog.

And I meditate on nothing at all.

I am in heaven.

Thursday, 1991

I am awake before dawn, peering into the darkness. The house is silent. I am lying on the couch in the living room, searching for a familiar morning sound or smell, but there are none. There is no sound of eggs and bacon frying, of the oven door opening and closing on biscuits. The percolator is silent. No scent of fresh coffee fills the house. From my place on the couch, I can see into the kitchen. Except for a tiny nightlight, it is dark.

This is when I realize how much my world is changing.

Granny is awake in her bed, too. I know this. Our bond is so strong, I *know* this. She has not come out to start the day. Instead, she is awake in her bed, prayerful and contemplative. Thousands of decisions have to be made, for Curtis is not with her.

Our Curtis died not 30 hours ago.

I glance at the clock on the mantle, but can only make out its shape in the dim light. I cannot see the face. Time has stagnated.

I was many miles away when Curtis died, though I knew it was "his time," as they say. He had been ill for a few months. Lung cancer. I was looking out the back window of my own house, many miles away. I gazed on a full moon, contemplating a future without him. In that moment of meditation, as he was about to leave, I heard a voice in my head. It said, "You'll need to say a few words about the man." I knew then I would be doing the funeral service, though there was no reason to expect to do so. I had never done one before, and no one had ever suggested I should. But I knew all the same.

Then, the phone rang. It was well after three in the morning when my father confirmed what I already knew. Curtis was gone.

Curtis died in this very room where I am now, though this fact does not bother me in the least. I am only a few feet from where Hospice set up a hospital bed a few weeks ago, a fact I find comforting, not disturbing. I feel close to him -- closer, for being here.

The bed has already been removed, of course. Curtis' body is gone, too, taken several miles away. But Curtis himself -- where is he now?

His energy is here, in this room, in this house. Certainly, he is in our hearts. But, there is that one question which faith alone can answer. To ask: "where is he?" is the same as asking "where is heaven?"

I do not know.

I believe there is a heaven, a something after this life. I just don't know what it is.

I decide to lie here, on this couch, wide awake, until there is at least a crack of sunlight, enough to see the face of the clock.

A couple of hours after receiving the news from Dad, Mom called. She explained that Granny and Curtis' preacher, an old family friend, was also very ill and not expected to live much longer. She went on to say that another minister they considered was sick with the flu. "Your grandmother wondered if you could do the service."

I said, "Yes."

Then Mom added, "She wants the service simple -- nothing fancy or long."

Of course, I thought. *That is exactly what*

Granny and Curtis would want: simplicity.

Granny and Curtis were married in 1930, the beginning of the Great Depression. They married in a barbershop near the county court house. To set up housekeeping, they sold the car they had used for "courting." Curtis walked to his job in the mines. And Granny? She milked a cow and kept some roosting hens. Each day she rode out the ridge on horseback selling eggs, milk, cream, and butter. Eventually, they built this house themselves, using lumber from a mining camp that was being dismantled.

Living a life of simplicity is not often easy -- it can, in fact, be very difficult to do. But simplicity is beautiful when you learn to appreciate the time it leaves for reflection, independence, and enjoying the people around you.

I again glance at the clock on the mantle. It is an unusual timepiece, an oval face with Roman numerals set in a half-circle of sculpted glass, like a moon rising up from a mountain lake. It reads 14 after three. This cannot be right. I squint to see the second hand -- frozen in place. The little clock has stopped.

I sigh, draw my feet up and over, and sit up on the edge of the couch. I have two jobs today: write the funeral service and attend tonight's wake. The funeral home calls it a "viewing," of course, but the country folk up here still call it a "wake." And today, "wake" is the proper word. My "education" tells me that "wake" comes from the necessary tradition of family members sitting up with the body, in their own parlors, their true homes, every night until the burial -- before the invention of the funeral "home" and embalming. But "wake" also conjures the image of ripples on the surface of a river -- the boat has pulled away, and we are left in the uneasy water. Our Curtis has left us, and we must find a new order to our lives. It will not be easy.

I stand up, stagger on morning legs into the kitchen, and find some homemade bread. Folk from all over the mountain, and beyond, have brought food, more food than the four of us could eat in a week.

"Four" should be "five."

I sit down to the table and look out the kitchen windows. Fog has wrapped the house in a thick and murky cocoon. I cannot see the mountain peak above the garden. I can barely see the grass on the other side of the sidewalk.

Slowly, the others defy the heavy gravity of the day and pull themselves out of bed: Granny first.

She smiles at me, nods her head, and blinks her eyes at me in that mischievous way she has greeted me a thousand and one times before. I smile back, and we share the moment with our eyes -- at least *this* will stay the same a few years longer.

Soon enough, Mom and Dad join us. We all sit at the table, quietly picking and eating from the food around us, chatting softly, laughing, grieving, dreading the hours ahead.

Eventually, we move on to our respective chores. After changing clothes, I walk through the kitchen, open the old, painted pine door, and head to the basement. The first step is a long one. The tread and its supporting part of the stringer broke away long before I was born. It is a detail I commit to memory, a fact that has been so present in this life it is taken for granted, thus easily forgotten. I eye the existing treads, their worn patterns and edges, their thicknesses. I examine the pull-string on the basement light. At the end of the string is a "pull" -- a metal wire that was used decades ago to dip eggs into dye for Easter. Curtis had found a use for something most people would throw away before the eggs had dried. "Use it up; wear it out; make do, or do without," a mountain maxim that seems quaint and antique in the disposable "real" world. But in the realm of the mountains of southern West Virginia it is still a way of life -- for now.

I peer into the coal bin. There is probably enough coal for this winter, but will Granny use it? She is very good at stoking the fire in the coal and wood furnace, of "laying it up" to keep the house warm all night, but . . . .

I make my way to the barn-style garage doors and glance up at the shotgun in its nest, in the joists. I remember Granny and the cow in her garden. Would she really have shot it had Curtis not been there to stop her?

I smile in spite of myself.

I also remember shooting the gun once myself; my first time shooting a shotgun. Curtis didn't think I would hit the target, an old coffee can, but I did.

I glance around the garage for a moment. I regret the fact that I never brought the old truck up here to work on with Curtis. I regret the fact that I never stayed for more than a week at a time.

I have many regrets.

Pushing open one carriage door, I step into the morning.

Dad is standing outside, out near the picket fence, alone in the fog. He is quietly smoking the day's first cigarette.

The fact that Curtis died of lung cancer hits me with this sight. But while it was true he smoked most of his life, Curtis also had Black Lung Disease from the years he worked in and around the mines. His skills as a mechanic kept him out of World War II; he served his country by keeping the machinery of the mines running, by getting coal to the factories building planes, Jeeps, and tanks. One of his first cousins once told me that working on the tipple machinery to get the coal out of the ground exposed you to more coal dust than the actual mining.

I shuffle over to Dad. We talk a few minutes, a quiet, loose morning chatter that leads us no-where in particular. It is as though we had both crawled out of a tent to the quiet solitude of nature, into a fog that envelopes us.

I take a deep breath, drawing in his smoke, the fog, and the scent of the large pine trees that line the picket fence. It is a sacred moment. I look to the east, hoping the sun will begin to burn through -- but, no.

I feel a compulsion to take a few more steps, out into the road -- to turn left and walk out the mountain ridge a few miles, maybe all the way to Boodge Harmon Flats, the one-time home of a bootlegger during Prohibition. I'd like to cut through the fields there, blend in with the fog, and disappear into the forest on the far side. Maybe if I believe hard enough that this were 500 years ago, I could walk for days and days and never see so-called "civilization."

But, I have work to do. Somber, yet loving work. I have the eulogy to write.

I walk back to my car and pop open the trunk of my red Sundance. I love this little car. We are a perfect match. Her name is "Caroline," but my wife, Kim, does not know this. Kim does not appreciate the way I name "things."

Last night, during the last hour of the trip here, to the mountain, Caroline and I made our way over desolate and winding roads. It had rained all day, and the thick fog was just rolling in. It was the first full day of winter and everything was dead and cold.

In a little town that appears on no map I know of, Caroline rolled over 75,000 miles on her odometer. Her warranty thus expired. That little fact made me feel even more alone and miserable. Warranties of all kinds were running out, guarantees a thing of the past.

When I finally walked in the backdoor and into the kitchen of Granny and Curtis' house, the first thing I did was hug Granny. I was surprised by the smile she gave me through her tears and the strength with which she clung to me. We had always been close, but our bond tightened even more in that moment. She whispered into my ear, "Our Curtis is gone."

Not "My," but "Our" -- the love this woman shares is astounding.

I looked over Granny's shoulder to my mother. Mom also managed a smile. She looked like Curtis for a brief moment. Dad patted me on the back as I hugged Mom. Words were useless, now; Granny had said it all.

I open Caroline's trunk and see my two briefcases. One is a "slender," leather job that strains at the stitching, ready to pop open, it is so full of papers and books. The other is a big, heavy, hard-shell Samsonite. It literary messed up my shoulder a few months ago, because it was so full. I had to see a doctor, get shots, take pills -- and carry it in my left hand for a while.

I recall how sad my great-grandmother, Granny Akers, looked when I held up my toy briefcase all those years ago. What would she say now?

I flop the shoulder ripping Samsonite over on its side. It usually carries research notes and books - stuff for my work toward a Ph.D. in medieval British literature. I shall be "Dr. Wolfe" in a few years. But, looking at medieval illustrations of Chaucer's pilgrims riding to Canterbury is as close as I get to a horse these days. I am losing touch with the mountain, with simplicity.

I flip the heavy latches on the Shoulder Ripper. There, instead of schoolwork, are a Bible, a clipboard with paper, and a bottle of Jim Beam. I had packed in a hurry, dumping the normal contents onto the floor of my study at 6:00 AM, before making the drive. The irony of these items sharing close quarters for the journey had been lost on me until now. The image of my great-grandmother's gun and Bible together in her store crosses my mind. A faint smile pushes at the corners of my mouth.

And I wonder, why am I thinking of her so much now? It is her 82-year-old son who has died, and for whom I need to say a few words to his friends and family. Why should Great-Granny Akers rise from the dead and haunt me today? Is her spirit here, now, on this mountain? Is it in me? Just how tightly linked are we to our ancestors? It is a question I have never really thought about before.

I pick up the Bible and clipboard, and close the Shoulder Ripper. I know I don't -- and won't -- need the whiskey. It is a new, sealed bottle I bought to calm my nerves if the grief gets to be too much. But my nerves are fine today. I carry a certain strength here. It comes from the ground, the dirt under my feet. This mountain is sacred. The energy of Akers Mountain flows in my veins.

This is what is meant by *home*.

Soon I am sitting on the enclosed front porch with the clipboard on my lap -- thinking, thinking about what to say. Granny wants short and simple. I find this difficult: short and simple are not exactly the common approach to the doctoral work I am doing. It is hard to simplify what I have to say as opposed to expounding mightily on this and that.   And too, my mind is cluttered. 1991 has been a hard year. There was The Gulf War with Iraq to liberate Kuwait -- and secure our oil interests.   My Aunt Mary, Dad's sister who sent me the toy brief case, is in a coma near her home in Florida. We don't know if she will make it or not. And of course there has been the "cloud" that follows all students, and the part-time job that is loaded with stress, and the novel I'm trying to write, and . . . .

I am happy about one thing, though: my wife, Kim, is pregnant.

This will be our second child.

We lost the first to a miscarriage last January, during the Gulf War.

We were as devastated by that as much as any other death of a loved one.

But, now, we are all hopeful. Deep down I know this child she now carries will live on in our lives for years to come. Kim and I already refer to the baby as "she." Though the ultrasound failed to reveal the sex of the baby, we just *know*. And I like that very much. We are even leaning toward the name "Katherine." "Katie."

Kim and "Katie" will join us tomorrow for the funeral. That will help. But, of course, Curtis will not get to see this child, and for that I am further saddened. It is important for these mountain folk to see the generations continue, to see the lines of family and traditions continue.

I recall a photo: me at about ten-months-old, Mom, Curtis (who is holding me) and Great-Granny Akers and Pampaw-with-the-chickens. Dad took the photo in the living room. Four generations.

And it strikes me now that I have done very little to hold onto those traditions myself. Instead of pursuing simplicity and a life with nature, I have a stuffy office in a university basement. I am pursuing some form of the American Dream, and I don't even know why.

And now, I realize I am not just grieving

for Curtis, but for a way of life. These Mountain People are a dying breed. I fear Curtis was far more like his parents than I will be like him or my own parents. I have drifted away.

I close my eyes to take this all in, and with the fatigue and emotions, I find myself imagining the full moon again.

Four generations -- and a fifth on the way. We have all seen the moon many times over this mountain -- the moon, the sun, the stars, the mountain, the trees, and the wind hold us together.

I remember something Curtis once said about the moon, and I begin writing his service. I decide to celebrate his life.

The fog is lifting.

Granny is at the doorway between the living room and the front porch, the glass clock in her hand. She asks me, if it's not too much trouble, to change the battery. I smile and say "of course," and take it from her hands -- hands that have prepared thousands of meals, worked the soil in the gardens, made butter, made quilts, and cared for flowers -- lots and lots of flowers. As I remove the back of the clock, she pulls a new battery from a pocket in her housecoat and hands it to me.

Granny looks out the windows at the dark clouds. "I reckon it'll be overcast all day," she says, though she seems to be looking at a world beyond this one.

Then it hits me, the time frozen on this clock is very close to the time of Curtis' death. Had this clock stopped at the moment his spirit left the flesh and bones? Or had it stopped 12, 24, 36 hours earlier? There are many documented cases of clocks stopping as someone in the house dies. Many see this as proof of an afterlife. Carl Jung even wrote about such "coincidences."

I look up at Granny. She would know. I start to ask her, but as I begin to formulate the words, a little bit of sunshine breaks through the clouds, almost due south. It is nearly noon. The sun is at the highest, thus closest point in its daily path over these mountains. Noon is the best chance for the sun to show itself on such a day. I can make out a bit of its outline among the branches of the pine trees. It lightens the profile of Granny's face. She has a beautiful look of serenity and sadness, a contentment of things being the way they are meant to be -- that everything happens for a reason.

I look back at the clock and the question has become unimportant.

I insert the fresh battery and set the clock for noon. Time lurches forward.

I put the old battery in my pocket, telling myself I will check it later, test my hypothesis.

Granny turns back to face me.

"Does it bother you that the burial will be on Christmas Eve?" she asks.

I pause for a moment, then reply, "No, not really. As much as you and Curtis loved Christmas, I actually find it fitting. It's good."

"You know, Curtis' brother, Basil, died at midnight between Christmas Eve and Day. Curtis and I were there."

"I remember." There is a little silence, then I add, "I guess they've been reunited at the same time of year -- almost 25 years later."

Granny smiles at me, "That does seem fitting, doesn't it?"

"Yes, it does."

The sunlight begins to fade. High noon has passed.

"Well," she says, "I best let you get back to your writing. But don't worry over it too much. I'm sure you'll do a fine job." Tears form in her eyes.

"I love you, Granny."

"I love you, too, Matt."

******

There is greenery on the casket, boughs of pine. I suggested this over the traditional spray of flowers. It is more fitting for a mountain man, a mountain man who loved Christmas.

Mom, Granny, and I are gathered at the head of the casket before the viewing begins.

Granny is the first to touch Curtis. She pats his hand as if to reassure him everything will be all right. She then gently touches and kisses his face. My legs are weak. This is the only moment that seems like a bad dream.

One of the first people to arrive to pay his respects is Curtis' cousin, Oscar. Like Curtis, Oscar is one of the last of the mountain men. He spent most of his life timbering, cutting props to hold up the roofs of the mines. He caught rattlesnakes with his bootlaces and gave the snakes to a local college to study. At one time he had the state record for catching the largest rattler.

He taught me how to find beehives simply by watching the bees in a field of wild flowers.

And he knows how to tell a great story, and how to laugh at one when he hears it. Typically, at previous wakes, you would find me, Oscar, Curtis, Dad, and a few other men standing off to one side talking and joking -- usually about the deceased. None of that is happening tonight.

Soon the room is filled with everyone from the mountains and all over the countryside. I find it hard to deal with the crush of people -- always have.

I step out on the front stoop for fresh air. There I find Dana Akers.

Dana is Mom's first cousin. He is also something of a storyteller and joker, but tonight he is subdued and talking quietly with a couple of men I don't recognize.   It was Dana's father, Curtis' brother, who died 25 years ago -- almost to the day.   I am sure this is as hard on Dana as it is the rest of us.

Dana looks a lot like Curtis, and I enjoy watching and listening to him talk.   Soon, the other two men go on into the "home." Dana and I talk a little, though we really don't know each other all that well. It is a little difficult to find things to say. There are moments of silence, but they are not awkward.

Suddenly he says, "I couldn't do what you're doing tomorrow." His tone is uneven.

"You mean the service," I reply.

"Uncle Curtis and Aunt Verna are two of the best people to ever walk this earth, and you know I ain't lying."

"No," I say, "You're right about that."

Dana pulls out his pipe and lights it. I find this familiar sight comforting. I also understand his concern about my ability to do a service without breaking down. The funeral director has similar concerns, though he was more blunt: "If you can't finish the service, who will take over?"

The funeral director is, of course, worried about the flow of the service, that everything go as planned. To him, it is a show that must be executed with proper order and decorum.

But Dana, I realize, is worried about *me*, not the ritual. Can *I* handle it.

"For one thing," I try to reassure him, "it's going to be short. The graveside service will be, too. Granny wants it that way. She doesn't want to listen to a long sermon -- so I'm doing this for her. I think Curtis would want it this way."

Dana takes a long draw on his pipe to consider what I've said, then he concurs with the decision: "Yeah, that's Curtis and Verna; that's exactly how they'd want it."

I look up at the sky. The clouds are finally breaking up. A few stars have turned out and the temperature will drop toward freezing. The moon will be up in a few hours.

The day is almost done.

"Well," Dana says, "I reckon I ought to

head home. But let me tell you something. You need to come and visit me. I'll take you out some roads on that old mountain that I'd bet money you've never seen before. I can show you a few things about *our* people."

"I'll try to do that sometime," I say -- knowing full well that as much as I'd like to, the chances are slim.

I watch him walk over to his truck, start the engine, and head down the road. I realize then that Dana is the last member of the family to know the family history, the secrets, and where the bodies are buried -- literally. I also realize, that at his younger age, he may well be the last mountain man in these parts.   And I wonder if I'll ever get to break away from my busy life to really spend time with him and learn more about who I am.

*****

As I get ready for bed, and the heavy load of tomorrow, I know full well that this is my last night in Granny and Curtis' house, the house I love so much.

After the service tomorrow, I will go with my wife back to her family (she and her father will drive up in the morning) and pretend to enjoy Christmas. This is the *right* thing to do -- but it is wrong for me.

After that?

The outside world is pushing in. The people on the mountain have changed in the past few years. Drug dealers are taking over. Houses have been burned to the ground. My Great-Great Uncle Robert was beaten and robbed in his own home. They even cut the phone lines. He was 99 years old and had weak legs. Curtis found him crawling along the road to use their phone. Uncle Robert never saw 100.

Tomorrow the house will be guarded, because homes are getting robbed when the thieves know people have headed to a funeral. A neighbor will sit on the front porch with a loaded shotgun across his lap.

Granny will have to move. Her beautiful, simple life is about to become a complex nightmare.

And, yes, I have thought of giving up my studies and moving here to be with Granny, to bring Kim and the baby to the mountain. To continue planting gardens in the black mountain soil. To travel these roads with Dana. To seek simplicity. To hear and feel Curtis and the other ancestors in the wind. To give my un-born daughter everything this mountain has to offer.

But I also know this will not work. My wife did not marry me with the notion I'd become a mountain man. It is not part of the plan.

I empty my pockets to get ready for bed and find the battery from the clock. The temptation to check it has faded. I know what I know. I know that Curtis is with us, and I need no proof of that. A battery tester would tell me nothing.

I go to the kitchen and toss the battery into the trash.

It is not my faith that is being tested here. It is me. What world do I belong in? What mask do I wear? Who am I?

I sleep, but I do not rest.

From the Celebration of Life For
ROY CURTIS AKERS
January 17, 1909 –
        December 22, 1991

It is natural at these times to search our hearts and minds for memories. One memory I have cherished these past few weeks is of a cool, summer night, sitting alone with Curtis out by the fire. I guess just about everyone in this room has spent time with Curtis by the fireplace behind his house. On this particular evening, Curtis and I were talking softly about life, family, and so on, when he suddenly leaned back and looked into the sky. I looked up as well. There was a big, clear, beautiful full moon. After a few moments of studying this wonderful sight, Curtis said, "I like a nice moon." Those words have stuck with me ever since.

Curtis enjoyed life's simple wonders; he enjoyed visiting with friends by a warm fire. He enjoyed milkshakes and peaches; he enjoyed his garden and his house on the mountain with the white picket fence. He enjoyed children and Christmas. By enjoying the simple things in life,

Curtis lived a far richer life than any man I know or ever expect to know. To me, Curtis lived a life that was the example of a Christian life; he valued life.

I don't know how many times over the past few years -- not days or weeks, but years -- I have heard people -- many of you are here today -- I have heard you say, "I would like to live like Curtis Akers" or "I wish my life were more like Curtis'," or more often, "I wish our life were as nice as Curtis and Verna's."

Today, I want to celebrate Curtis's life by challenging each of us to take time out for the simple yet so valuable things in life. As we leave today and go to our Christmases, let's each search for those meaningful things which will make our lives richer. As we enter a new year, let's make time for children, for family, for friends, for peaches -- for nice moons. For by doing this, not only will we celebrate Curtis Akers' wonderful life, but we will find ourselves closer to God as well."

From the Graveside Celebration of Life for
VERNA HONAKER AKERS
August 29,1910 –
    October 14, 2000

We find ourselves here today to celebrate the life of a uniquely beautiful woman, Verna Akers. Like her husband, Curtis, she believed in simplicity and humility. It was her request that today's service be limited to a simple celebration here in this natural setting. It is further fitting that it is a warm, October afternoon with the trees in full color.

I am sure that most, if not all, of us here would agree that Verna was, and still is, a spiritual anchor for her communities and family. No matter how far we drifted from our spiritual centers, no matter how often our prayer time was washed to the side in our busy lives, Verna was there praying for us and holding us close with her steady and abundant love. She prayed for us continually. Granny taught me more about faith than anyone else, through her words and her actions. She lived her faith.

I, alone, can think of countless times when

her faith helped me. There was the time I was seriously ill in the hospital, and her presence gave me strength. There was also the time a very small child in the community had died. Granny told me we should pray for the little girl and her family. I asked her why God would allow a child to die. Granny answered that she did not know, but -- "God has a reason for everything." Now, I have heard that answer dozens of times in my life, but I have never heard it expressed with as much conviction and faith as when Verna Akers said it. She had no doubt but what God has a purpose for each of us.

I know most of you here could tell similar stories. At one time or another, I have heard many of you tell stories of how Verna's faith and love have had a profound and beautiful affect on you. In deed, Verna Akers has always been there for us, and it is my belief, that she will continue to be there for us in the days ahead if we keep our hearts open to her faith.

Like Granny, we should remember that God created this world, and though we may not understand everything that happens, we should accept there is a reason for everything.

And today, we should be happy that Verna Akers has gone to be with God. And most importantly, we should allow her life to shine as an example for each of us.

As we each leave this place and return to our hectic lives, let us follow the example set by Curtis and Verna Akers to live our lives in faith and simplicity, for it is in such a life that we may truly find heaven.

What I Did On My Fall Vacation
In The Mountains With Cousin Dana Akers:
A Statistical Report to My email List
October 30, 2003

Number of hours spent in the mountains: 110
Number of hours I spent in a four-wheel drive
    truck with Cousin Dana: 22
Number of those hours all four wheels were
    engaged: 7
Number of graves I saw containing dead
    ancestors: 15
Number of graves I saw containing live
    ancestors: 0

Earliest date on the tombstones: 1853
Total number of country cemeteries visited: 4
Number of unmarked Indian graves visited: 3
Hours spent driving along the New River: 3
Hours spent driving along the New River with
    the four-wheel drive engaged: 2

Estimate, in miles, of the width of the river at its
    widest point at Parrot, VA: 5/8
Number of minutes an actual parrot sat on my
    shoulder that same day: 15
Number of minutes it took the parrot to remove
    my hat and glasses for me: 1
Number of injuries sustained on the entire trip: 1
    (the parrot bit me)

Number of waterfalls spotted: 4

Approximate number of deer spotted: 32

Approximate number of wild turkey: 18

Number of empty Wild Turkey bottles: 1

Ratio of buzzards to dead deer: 7:1

Number of clean deer ribs I saw in a buzzard huddle: 6

Number of dead opossums on paved roads: 7

Number of dead opossums on unpaved roads: 0

Number of slow crows lying dead beside dead opossums: 1

Number of times "I smelled me a skunk": 1

Number of times I heard the word "Ain't": 196

Number of times I used the word on my last day there: 2

Number of mountain hermit shacks passed: 2

Number of times I have watched the movie *Deliverance*: 3

Number of people I saw who had "Deliverance eyes": 6

Odds they were kin of mine: 1:1

Number of churches with the word "Deliverance" in their names: 2

Number of "white lightning" stills sighted: 1
Percentage of mountain folk who use the words
        "White Lightning": 0%
Number of bar fights I saw: 0
        (no vacation is perfect)

Number of pounds I gained on country food: 5
Number of beautiful, country girls I fell in love
        with: 4
Number of actual, working phone numbers I got
        from those girls: 0
Number of hours I'll spend in the gym before my
        next trip: 2,387

Minutes I spent walking on a marked trail: 15
Minutes I spent walking alone OFF the marked
        trail: 98
Minutes I was lost: 0

Number of mud spots I got on my new denim
        jacket: 13
Chance that any one spot came from the places of
        my ancestors: 75%
Total number of family secrets passed down to
        me: 4

Number of times it struck me that my stubbornness, lack of respect for authority, and my fierce need for independence come to me naturally: over 15

Number of times I realized we are royally screwing up our planet: Every minute I was in the woods.

Friday, 2008

Mom and I glide over a gentle mountain pass and slip into a narrow valley. We are between our home and *home*.

It is a soft, sunny October morning. Clear, blue skies hang over the fall colors like a shroud billowing down from heaven. The gold and red leaves of the hardwood trees frame the highway, and I feel the weight of civilization tumble into our wake. We skip through patches of shade and sunlight like a flat rock on the surface of a pond. I feel the differences in temperatures on my arms and hands.

It is as though the seasons are trading places at this very moment.

And perhaps they are.

I look over at my mother: the sight of the

mountains has already erased much of the pain from her face. She is beautiful.

She turns to look at me. We smile. I catch images of Granny and Curtis on her face in the flickering light.

We cross yet another bridge over yet another hollow, and begin climbing another mountain. The sun is in my eyes.

But it is a dark day all the same, a day full of sorrow.

The past few years have been unkind.

Mom and I are traveling to the mountain, though we can't really go home again.

After Curtis' death, the world turned up-side-down.

Granny sold the house to a family she knew and eventually moved into an apartment we added to Mom and Dad's house. We called it the "Granny Pad." There she lived, comfortable and content -- but missing Curtis, the mountain, and her way of life. The world of suburbia was too busy, too complicated. The Ohio River Valley weather was too hot and unforgiving, the soil tough and dead. Nothing grew well. The busy, busy neighbors with their fast-track lives zoomed past her in their new SUV's, a fog of exhaust and exhaustion lingering behind them.

It was as though Granny had moved from

the 1930s to the 21st century in the blink of an eye.

And, in confession, my own fast-track life may have buffaloed her more than anything else. I was jetting off to do research in England, flying all over the United States to present papers at "important" conferences, interviewing for teaching positions at universities from California to Massachusetts.

Ironically, one of the reasons I had gone back to school was to get a teaching position at a small college nestled somewhere in the mountains. But that had turned out to be a pipedream. Upon becoming Dr. Wolfe, over three hundred people were applying for 30 jobs in my field. In the end, I was reduced to teaching part-time in the same stinking river valley I had once escaped.

My wife told me my education was a waste. There were other, more serious problems in my marriage as well.

Now I am divorced. Nine years.

Now Granny is with Curtis again, and I live in the "Granny Pad."

Mom fell and shattered her right knee and tibia three years ago. Surgery and six months of physical therapy helped, but it still pains her. She also has arthritis throughout her body.

The price she will pay for this one-day trip? A week of agony in bed.

Dad has Parkinson's disease now and doesn't even feel like making the trip.

So it is just Mom and me, in a Jeep, driving in silence. I have not named the Jeep; rather, it has not yet revealed its name to me.

Mom and I are heartbroken -- utterly and thoroughly.

Just over a year ago, my daughter, Katie, began to turn on us. That's the only way I know how to put it. She seemed to resent us for some reason and spent less and less time with us until, finally, she estranged herself from our dwindling family. We do not know why, though it is clear she has no use for our way of looking at the world. More specifically, she seems to resent my value of simplicity. That and Mom's value of love and acts of kindness, her love and respect for simple gifts from the earth -- like rocks and daisies.

It is as though, dare I say it -- it is as though Katie has rejected our mountain heritage, as though she has rejected the mountain itself, though she has visited it several times. I have seen the wondrous effect of it in her eyes and voice.

We pull off the interstate and begin

driving out a rambling two-lane highway. My mind often flashes back to riding these same roads when I was a child. Today I think about the old Ford truck that was part of my first memories of coming up here. That truck is still with us, so to speak. Dad kept it.

It is in a thousand pieces, scattered throughout my garage. I dismantled it. Yesterday, I began grinding the rust off the frame -- the restoration has begun, and I wonder if I should put seat belts on it when the time comes.

In the State of West Virginia, you do not have to put seatbelts on antique vehicles -- thus I have the freedom of one small choice. Odd that such a freedom should feel like a luxury.

But this is our inheritance from the industrial revolution: We create things, like cars, to make our lives "better." When those inventions kill us, rather than reject them, we create new technologies to save us, and when those technologies kill us, we create more. We call this process *Progress*.

My father's Parkinson's is generally believed to be caused by industrial toxins which pull a genetic trigger which, in turn, screws up the central nervous system. Parkinson's Disease may not have existed before factories. This is progress.

My mother's form of arthritis and a host of other auto-immune diseases we now face, are related to the stresses of living in this modern world. This is progress.

For over 16 years, I have loved my daughter more than all else in this world, and now, considering her rejection of me and my values, her rejection of the life symbolized by these mountains, it seems I have lost her to commercialism and materialism. This is progress.

It is that simple.

I drive into a small cemetery. When I get close to the gravesites we seek, I pull off the narrow road as best as I can and shut off the engine -- Mom and I are trapped in silence. The sun is as high as it's going to get today.

I remember that I regret never learning a few steps of the Charleston.

Eight years ago this month, we buried Granny next to Curtis. For the service, we placed one of her quilts on the casket. The quilt rustled softly in the warm October breeze, a moment of peace before I began the service.

A friend once told me that leading the service of a loved one lost is a precious gift.

This is true.

As Granny died, Mom held her left hand. When the hospice nurse announced the passage complete, Mom pulled Granny's hand to her own tear-streaked face. A moment later, Mom turned to us -- Dad, my cousin Anna, and me -- and, through tears and astonishment, she said, "Mother's hands smell like her flowers."

This is truth.

Mom and I step from the Jeep and approach the simple headstone.
I expect Mom to break down into tears and grief. I am prepared for it, but she is surprisingly stoic. We stand graveside in silence for a few moments. Then we talk softly about our trials. We talk about Katie, and September 11th, 2001, and a world that seems to have lost all common sense. Mom does tear up a little, but I am not sure for which loss she grieves.

Then she says, "I know this will sound gross, but I can't help wondering what your grandmother's body looks like now."

I take a deep sigh and reply, "I think a lot of people wonder that sort of thing at times. I've done it myself."

Mom is quiet for a few moments, so I add: "Many cultures eventually gather the bones of their ancestors and store them in places of honor. And don't forget that for centuries, the

Catholic Church has kept the bones of saints as holy relics."

Mom smiles a little bit. We have both thought of Granny as a saint.

Mom says, "I would like to see her bones."

"Me, too," I reply meekly. I am shocked, not by what she says, but by the fact I was thinking the exact same thing. Maybe Mom and I are soul mates. Dad seems to think so.

Mom approaches the headstone and slips two small pieces of paper under it, one under the name "Verna" and one under the name "Curtis." I do not know if these are prayers or notes, nor do I ask. I find the scene touching, an act of miraculous trust. My mother never ceases to amaze me with her gentle grace.

Soon we are back on the road and headed into the town of Princeton. It is the center of activity for the region. We circle the courthouse, pass the barbershop where Granny and Curtis were married, and make our way to a restaurant for lunch with several of our cousins: Dana and his sisters.

Since that bleak night of Curtis' wake, Dana and I have gotten to know each other quite well. After my divorce, I took him up on the offer to drive me all over the mountains and show me things about our family. He kept his promise.

Over the past few years we have made several treks in four-wheel drive trucks, exploring passes one could pretend were roads. He has shown me the cemetery where our Cherokee great-great grandparents are buried. He has told me hundreds of stories about our family and about life on Akers Mountain from the time the Akers clan first settled there. And, more than I ever would have anticipated, he has shown me something more about myself.

So, when we all meet up at the Shoney's Restaurant (Dana's favorite place to eat and shoot the breeze), Dana and I sit at one end of the table, his sisters sit around the other, and Mom sits in between. It is a typical country arrangement of men and women for such occasions -- only I notice something different here. Dana and I discuss politics, weather, the restoration of my old truck, and nuggets of family history. His sisters talk about doctors' visits, TV shows, food, and their grandchilren (Katie is conspicuously absent from this conversation). And Mom is straining to be in on both conversations at once. She is breaking the traditional boundaries.

I have heard Dana complain -- repeatedly -- that no one in the family really wants to know its history, not to the extent he knows it.

At one point in our meal, the sisters even tease him about "going on with those old stories." Meanwhile Mom chats with them, but every once in awhile, like when Dana talks about how Grandpa used a mowing scythe, Mom's attention drifts over to our end of the table.

This is when I realize just how rare *we* are becoming. Dana's sisters are all about the present and their connection to the activities of worldly realities. They and their families see the world as more or less normal, and there is nothing wrong with that. I suppose this is the same divide that has drawn Katie away from me.

On the other side of this divide, Dana, Mom, Dad, and I are struggling to hold onto our connections with the past. I now suspect one reason Dad fell in love with Mom was his attraction to this world, even if Curtis never did introduce him as kin. Dad was always "Marlene's husband," and he was happy to have edged into this reality at least that much.

My two post-divorce girlfriends have complained that I dwell too much on the past. On one hand I am tempted to rebel, to point out there is a vast difference between living in the past and learning from it. But that is *only* a valid, logical argument, and there is something more fundamental about the way some of us see the past. For us the past is alive, just as the rocks and the mountains and the rivers are alive. Our ancestors are alive. Calendars and wrist watches make no sense in this reality. Stories are alive, and we learn with them. But it is one reason my relationships never seem to last.

Dana tells me about a minor war he is waging with local politicians: "Let me tell you something, Matt. Fighting the folks at the courthouse is like getting into a pissing match with a skunk. Even if you win, you're gonna lose."

Even as I laugh, I realize that my parents and I are fighting the same war as Dana. We are fighting greed, corruption, shallowness, materialism, and waste. We are fighting a losing battle against a modern belief system based on values I find nowhere in the natural world.

All of Curtis' siblings and cousins are gone now -- even Oscar-rattlesnake-catcher, and I look at Dana and realize that he is the last mountain man I know or will ever know.

It is a disturbing thought, and I lose my appetite.

After taking leave of our cousins, Mom and I drive over winding, rolling two-lane highways. The warm afternoon sun bakes my arms. It feels good, but I am still chilled by the idea that the world I know is ending.

As we climb up the mountain road, I roll down my window a couple of inches, and the fresh air perks us up. There is hope on the breeze.

When we reach the summit, I pull off the road and stop at the spot of the Akers' Store. There is nothing much to see. The remnants from the fire have finally been trucked off to the salvage yard. The earth has been smoothed over. To newcomers driving by this place, the store never existed.

I try to gauge where I stood all those years ago, showing Great-Granny Akers my little briefcase. I recall her lifeless eyes and the shadow of concern on her face.

I don't have any briefcases with me today. I gave one away, and the Shoulder Ripper sits in my closet -- full of childhood mementoes.

Mom and I say very little. I suppose she is navigating her own memories of what once was. I suppose too, this is why we have come so far.

The memories of our childhoods are planted in the rich earth to bloom whenever our hearts desire. Visiting these places nurtures those flowers.

After a while, I sense Mom is finished here.

"Ready," I ask. My voice shatters the silence. Maybe I am rushing her.

But she answers, "Yes," and I start the engine.

We leave the highway behind us and make our way out a lightly graveled road. Then, after passing a field and a crooked walnut tree where a small church once stood, we turn down off the mountain ridge onto a narrow, deep-rutted dirt road. We stay on this for about a half-a-mile until we come to a slight bend. Mom recognizes the place, even without landmarks, even though it's been many, many years since she was last here.

She gazes on a gentle slope above the road. It is covered with small trees, many of them already losing their leaves. Somewhere under the forest floor, under decades of leaves and branches and grass and plants is the foundation of a one-room schoolhouse. Mom taught here during her first year of teaching. She walked to school every day, pumped the water, rang the bell.

She was a one-room schoolteacher at a time before TV and Wal-Mart. For the kids she taught here, a paper napkin with decorations for this holiday or that was a glorious treasure. Imagine it if you can. The children would hug her so much, Granny had a hard time getting sooty handprints off Mom's white blouses. And before the school system reached this hollow, the older children taught the younger ones and thus taught themselves.

Imagine a school where learning is fun and loving.

But again, Mom is stoic. I am a little surprised, maybe even disappointed by her reaction. But I can hear the memories rustling through her mind.

After a few minutes, I look down the hill on the opposite side of the road. A thin, gray stream of smoke is drifting up lazily. There are no houses in that area that I know of. The smoke is probably coming from a still. Yep. Even in 2008 people are making their own moonshine whiskey in these mountains. I smile and think that maybe some things will never change here after all.

But I am in no mood to meet up with the still's owners -- or the barrel end of a shotgun, so I ease off the clutch and mosey on past the school site.

We start up a small incline. The wheels slip on some loose rocks and dirt, so I engage the four-wheel drive. We are in the boonies now. If we get stuck, it's a long walk to find help. The bumps and the rocks and the washouts are jostling us about. I try to take it as easily as I can, but I can almost feel the pain of Mom's arthritis.

Finally, we burst out onto a wider, dirt road. A good road, an even road. *The* road. I turn west. Granny and Curtis' house is only a half-a-mile away now.

Of course, it doesn't really look like their house anymore. The bottom half has been painted a different color. Different curtains hang on the enclosed front porch. And -- the picket fence is all but gone. It was a lot of work to keep up, so the new owners have let it go. I have watched it rot down for 16 years now. All that remain are a few pieces of the paintless posts, sticking up from the earth and pine needles.

And somehow this seems natural. This feels right. Everything returning to the earth. I am sad and happy to see it go.

As we approach, I spot three children playing in the front yard where I once played. I ease past the house and pull into the driveway of the little house next door, where Ellen and Verlin have lived for so long now. Their children are grown. I find myself wanting to see Bear, the black German Shepherd Curtis liked to groom with the broom, but, of course, Bear died long ago, too.

As I shut off the engine, Ellen comes out of the house -- surprised and pleased to see us. Mom steps out of the Jeep. She is shaky and tired. I suspect this is Mom's last trip to the mountain, to southern West Virginia.

As I get out, I watch Mom and Ellen approach each other. They hug -- and Mom breaks down. The tears roll, and her head drops onto Ellen's shoulder.

Ellen looks at me in shock, "What's wrong!?" Her voice is full of alarm. She thinks some tragedy has just come to pass.

I smile to her in a frail, crooked smile -- fighting back my own tears, "Mom's homesick. We both are."

Ellen does her best to console Mom for the next few minutes.

I try to focus on the scene around me, the two houses, the mountain peak where I once flew a kite with Dad, the hollow where I went sleigh riding with my cousins, the gardens, the trees I climbed -- and napped under.

The three children who had been playing in the yard are now standing beside us. It turns out they are Ellen's grandchildren. They are a beautiful sight with their messy hair and a little black mountain dirt on their faces -- they are, I think, exactly what children should look like. They remind me of myself. And for the second time today, I feel a little hope for the future. The mountain is a sacred place, and it is part of them.

John, their father, walks up, and I can't believe how tall he is. Ellen tells us Verlin is off hunting, and we visit for several minutes. For a fleeting moment, we are home.

*****

I navigate the winding road off the mountain, and Mom is soon asleep.

I have a small epiphany.

When Curtis died, the transition forced me to unveil the dual life I was trying to lead. I no longer had the mountains to escape to, to reaffirm my genuine self, or my values. Instead of accepting such a loss, I tried to live a lie.

I can no longer do that, yet I see no clear way to get back to what I once knew. As I pull onto the interstate, I realize just how much the world is against me.

*****

I sit on the edge of my bed. My stomach is

in a knot. My heart is gravely, perhaps fatally wounded. I have little incentive to go on with my life. This is not a suicidal moment -- this is an acknowledgement of everything and everyone, including my own daughter, that I have lost over the past two decades. The grief literally causes pain in my heart. It feels as though a large piece of me has been plucked from the center of my chest. I did not know that emotional loss could cause such intense physical pain. I question that damned saying: "It is better to have loved and lost than to never have loved at all." I try to hold onto what Granny taught me so long ago: There is a purpose for everything.

The image of Granny and Curtis' gravesite drifts to the surface of my grief. For the first time in my life I understand the concept of holy relics, of placing the cleansed bones of a loved one in a safe and sacred place.

Yes, I want to see her bones. It is true. I want to hold them.

Yet, I know my grandmother's spirit and energy are alive and present. I feel them from time to time. And I feel how they have intermingled with that universal power I call God. And still, I ache to be with her.

This must be what is meant by divine love, a love I wish I could share more freely with others.

I stand up and open my closet door. I reach in and pull a bundle from the top shelf. It is a quilt I keep in a pillowcase for safekeeping.

I pull the quilt out of the case and gently unfold it on my bed. This is one of the several quilts Granny made for me. This is the one she was making in the attic room, the scene I tried so hard to capture in my mind, because even then I knew that beautiful world could not last forever. This is the quilt with pieces of her plaid summer dress that I liked so much. This is the quilt she made for my wedding gift, though my wife and I never used it -- thank goodness. This is a quilt that should be shared with someone who accepts me for who I really am.

I crawl into bed and pull the quilt into my arms, up to my face. I clutch it with love. I recall the last lines of the service I gave for Granny: "As we each leave this place and return to our hectic lives, let us follow the example set by Curtis and Verna Akers to live our lives in faith and simplicity, for it is in such a life that we may truly find heaven."

I have lost my way.

I sleep with the quilt in my arms, like a four-year-old clinging to his blanket, for this quilt is my only comfort.

Saturday, 2010

"They's only three of us Mountain Boys left," Dana says. "And one of them isn't doing too good these days."

So he is *keeping count,* I think. *Three men left who understand these mountains.* It's a sobering thought.

Dana and I have been riding over mountain roads for almost three hours now. We passed Granny and Curtis' house long ago, and we are at the far eastern end of a ridge. It is a wonderful spring Saturday, and he is quizzing my memory. As we pull up to an area, I tell him the stories he's told me on our past excursions. I mix in some stories Curtis used to tell me, one or two even Dana hasn't heard before. Hundreds of years of mountain history awaken wherever we venture. Time does not exist as some linear, factory punch-clock out here among the pines, oaks, and blooming rhododendron. Time is vibrant, alive -- flowing in all directions.

Dana turns onto another road, and we immediately begin to ease down the side of the mountain.

For a moment, my thoughts turn to my daughter, Katie. It has been three years since we last spent genuine time together. It has been two years since I last saw her or heard her voice. She is dead to me. Even if she returned to me today, things would never be the same.

Making this trip is a bit of a triumph, a step back to normalcy, back to self-preservation. The worst thing that could possibly happen to me has happened, and I am fighting to stand up again.

Dana understands this. His own daughter, Cathy, was killed in a car accident when she was about eighteen years old. She was his only child. Dana also saw things in The Korean War that no man should have to witness. He has told me the stories, and he has told me about the nightmares that still haunt him. And so, we travel these roads with our burdens and find peace in the forest.

As we round a small bend, I look at my right hand. The only physical sign of my losses is a tremor in the thumb, though when the stress gets to be too much, the entire hand shakes. My hand hurts a great deal as well. In the past year I have been unable to play my guitars, type on the computer, or write my rough drafts in longhand. I can't work on the old truck. The simple act of writing a check is torture. The hand never relaxes. It is always prepared to create a fist. My jaw is always locked up. I have gained a lot of weight.

Grief has nearly killed me.

Deep down I wonder if I have developed Parkinson's Disease like Dad.

But being out on isolated roads is healing. Nature is healing. That observation is obvious and remote at the same time in our modern, high-tech world. More than once I have lamented that, thanks to my education, I have lots of knowledge, but my lack of time in nature has left me barren of the wisdom these mountain people have.

Dana is telling me some of the history of this road, because it is one I've never been on before. Even by our standards, it is not much of a road. It is narrow and overgrown, full of large rocks and stones. From time-to-time we come to washed out areas that make it virtually impossible to continue. This leaves me, the passenger, on the valley side of the road, and the tires on my side of the truck roll mere inches away from the edge.

At one washout, I assume we'll have to give up, put the truck in reverse, and back up the road a couple of miles (there are few places to turn around). But Dana dares the earth to hold, and on we go. I just smile -- it really doesn't matter much to me what happens. I am along for the ride and intend to take whatever comes our way.

A couple of slow and scenic miles later, we come to another bend in the road, and as is often the case, the road crosses a ravine in the bend. Or does the ravine cross the road? I'm not sure.

We stop to get out, stretch our legs, and size up the situation.

Yes, there is a drainpipe sticking out on the lower side. But there is also a pool of water and frogs on the upper side of the road. Not much drainage going on here. And, too, the road here was created by packing loose dirt in the ravine and around the apparently plugged-up pipe. This is obviously not the same as driving on a roadbed cut out of a mountainside.

And did I mention that it had rained the night before? Buckets.

Water has washed across the road leaving it spongy. And, in fact, the heavy rain washed away part of the road so that said road is now narrowest in the bend.

I start to suggest we turn back, but Dana is ahead of me: "I kind of wanted to see if the old bridge has ever been replaced."

"What old bridge?" I ask.

"There used to be a bridge on down this road a piece. The man who built it got angry one day, and took all the planks off of it."

Now, if you are questioning why anyone would drive five or six miles down a country road to see if a bridge has been replaced, and knowing that if it isn't you'll merely have to drive back, in reverse for much of the way, you've missed the point of Appalachian adventures. I am proud to say Dana's plan makes perfect sense to me.

With that, Dana heads back to the truck, "I reckon we can get across."

I crawl in and consider using my seatbelt/shoulder strap, but I decide that is against the rules of this adventure, and it hangs slack beside me.

Dana puts the truck in gear, and we ease up to the ravine-road intersection. I feel the truck sink just a little into the soggy soil. But no matter. Even if a wheel starts spinning, this is a four-wheel drive truck. The other three will pull us out.

The front wheels pass over the plugged pipe. So far, so good. Dana starts cutting hard on the steering wheel, and I suddenly have this feeling that the truck's wheelbase just stretched out about 40 feet behind us. It's like we suddenly became a semi and trailer and there's no way we'll make this cut.

I lean forward to peer into the mirror. *No*, I think, *there's the right rear wheel. We have just enough room. But -- wait, the ground is awfully soft and --*

And I start to tell Dana to stop, but the words won't form, the lips won't move, and the next sinking feeling I get is of the road caving into the ravine and the right rear wheel following it. We bump onto the road and abruptly stop.

This is how to get a four-wheel drive truck hung up on an unknown road in West Virginia.

There is no cussing, yelling, or kicking of tires. No gnashing of teeth or renting of clothes. Just a frog burping in the pond beside us.

Dana puts the truck into park (as if it'll go anywhere), and sighs ever so slightly. We again step out to look over the situation. There's not much to see: the truck is hung up on the frame. It's not going anywhere without a tow truck. Even though we know better, we check our cell phones: no signal. We look around another moment or two, and, without discussion, we start walking back up the road. Up the side of the mountain.

It's as simple as that.

After about 200 yards, Dana asks the same question I'm thinking: "How far do you reckon it is to that little farm house we saw up on the ridge there?"

"About 3 or 4 miles," I reply, "or an hour at the rate we're walking."

He laughs at this and thus offers his agreement.

The next hour and fifteen minutes is a wonderful mix of walking and random conversation, of looking at the fresh greens of spring and exploring mountain philosophy.

"The only thing a man needs is a horse and a dog," Dana says as we approach the washout we barely navigated a while ago.

"You're probably right," I reply.

"You know I am," he says, "When I had that pony and dog of mine, we'd come out this way just about every week. Visiting folks. Maybe do a little trading. Just riding all over these mountains."

The implication is his sense of freedom.

But I also wonder if he's testing me again, wanting to know what I plan to do with the rest of my life. Or, as his sisters may want to know, will I ever marry again?

It has been 11 years since I left my marriage, 7 years since I was in a relationship. Heck, it's been 3 years since I was even on a real date.

I reply to Dana by telling the truth, without really replying at all, "A horse and a dog would be nice. I've been thinking the same thing. But a woman would be nice, too. If I ever find a woman half as good as Granny was, I'll marry her."

Without missing a step, he shoots back, "You might as well stop looking now, 'cause there ain't no such woman."

And that's probably true.

We stop talking as we pace up a particularly steep stretch of road.

In about a year, Dana and I will reach two of the big milestones of life -- he will turn 80, and I will turn 50.

It occurs to me that a fifty-year-old man

without a wife or child is a dangerous person in this society.

I don't mean I'll become a terrorist or take out a post office. But there is a part of me prepared to move into these mountains and disappear. I have had that notion ever since, well -- ever since Curtis died. Maybe I should become a mountain hermit, hunt ginseng for a few coins to rub together, and live off of the land. Or "live off the grid," as younger men have started calling it. There are people doing this. Dana and I are not the only ones repulsed by the modern world.

Or, at least, maybe I should have a small farm -- with a horse and a dog. Dana does not know this, but I have started looking into horseback riding lessons.

My desire to escape back to the mountains has always been with me, but what makes it different this time is I have started yielding to the temptation. The temptation to become a sage of sorts. Maybe a mystic. Or an ecstatic. These are the real threats to western civilization.

Dana and I reach a place where the road begins to level off. I know where we are, and as we get closer to the farmhouse, I find we are getting a little tense. After all, we're in the middle of nowhere and about to ask strangers for help.

"I sure wish I'd brought my gun with me," Dana says, apparently sharing my own thoughts.

I had assumed he had. Out of curiosity I ask, "Do you have a conceal and carry permit?"

"Sure I do. It's called the Bill of Rights."

I smile and shake off the tension I feel. Freedom is all I ask for.

Soon we reach the gravel driveway up to the little house.

We are no more than 25 feet up the driveway when Dana snorts, "No one's home."

"What makes you say that?"

"Look at these tire tracks." He points down to a little spot of gray mud. Sure enough there are tire tracks, but --

He knows what I'm going to ask and replies before I can ask it, "See, the ones headed out are overtop the ones headed in."

I see, but I don't see. Is he serious? Is he really tracking cars? At first I think he's trying to pull one on me. It sounds like some bad Indian movie, "Yes, Squanto, Big Ram truck with Goodyear tires. Headed west, 3, maybe 4 hours ago."

But I look at Dana's face. He's serious.

Still, we keep walking toward the house. No, *I'm* still walking to the house. Dana heads for a grassy spot under the shade of an oak tree: "I'm telling ya, no one's home."

And he is right. I stop in my tracks, look at the little house, and *know* he is right. If anyone were home, they'd be peering out the window at us by now.

I walk back and join him in the shade.

We are quiet for a moment. It is at least another two miles to the next road -- then what? There isn't a house there, just an intersection.

We check our phones. I have a signal, but whom do we call?

We hem and haw for a few minutes, then we do what any other mountain men would do. We call AAA Road Service.

OK. I call. I'm the wimp with the magical get-out-of-trouble-free card.

I dial.

"Hello, Triple-A, how can I be of assistance?"

"Uh, well, my cousin and I got our truck stuck on a country road. We need a wrecker to get it out."

"Are there any injuries or other vehicles involved?"

"No. Just the two of us."

"And you're stuck in a ditch by the road."

"Well, technically, we're stuck in a ravine across a road -- part of the road caved in on us."

"Are you blocking traffic?"

"Uh ma'am. We haven't see another vehicle in three hours."

"But you are blocking the road?"

"Well, yes. But the road has caved in -- so it's blocked for good now. As I said it's a country road, and . . . . "

"Are you on the pavement?"

"Uh ma'am, there is no pavement there."

"So you managed to pull off the pavement?"

"Um-- in a manner of speaking, yes."

"How far off the pavement are you."

"About five miles."

Silence.

"Sir, this isn't a prank call, is it?"

"Ma'am, I promise. We're on a dirt road in Southern West Virginia. We are in the middle of a forest. We walked four miles just to get this cell signal. We need a wrecker."

"Why a wrecker?"

"Because we need winched AND lifted out of the place. A rollback can't really do that."

"What color is the truck?"

"Excuse me?"

"Sir, we need to know the color so the tow truck driver will be able to spot you as he drives by."

And on and on it went. I felt like I was 1930 placing a call to 2010. Here I was on a beautiful little farm on a beautiful spring day talking to a woman somewhere near Pittsburgh who was sitting under fluorescent lights in cubicle hell. We were only about 5 hours apart geographically, but we were in entirely different worlds, cultures, and times.

Finally the interrogation ends, I give her directions and my cell phone number, and remind her once again that we need a wrecker -- not a rollback.

By now Dana is stretched out on the grass. Life is good.

I, on the other hand, want to explore.

I walk up to a white wooden fence and look over a pasture and the ridge beyond it. Soon, a black calf wanders up over the ridge and looks at me with a sweet face. "Come on," I call to it. But it looks at my hands and sees no food -- no reason to walk over to me. I call a couple more times and finally it walks a little closer, but still sees empty hands, and proceeds to graze on a large tuft of grass.

The sky is a spring blue, the grass and

trees vibrant green. I am lost in the scene. And after awhile, I notice something: for the first time in nearly a year my hand and jaw are fully relaxed, my thumb is steady as rock. I reflect on this a while and can reach only one conclusion: I belong in the mountains.

After a bit, Dana and I are restless. We decide to walk back out to the road and walk up the mountain until we meet the tow truck. Dana suggests that the sooner we find the truck, the less time the driver has to change his mind about coming down this road.

As we walk back out the driveway of the farmhouse, Dana says, "Whoever ran the grader over this road didn't know a thing about how to do it."

"That's because it wasn't a grader," I say. "It was a bulldozer. See the dozer tracks in the ditch there."

Dana looks at the ditch and then looks at me with a big smile. Maybe there's hope for me after all.

But now the fun begins, or at least Dana and I think of it as fun: Triple A sends us a rollback, not a wrecker.

The driver, a young muscular man with a fair tan, is friendly enough, and when Dana snorts something about how we asked for them to send a wrecker, the driver just shrugs his shoulders, and mutters, "they didn't tell me."

So we climb up into the cab, Dana in the middle and me once again on the steep valley side of the road. I look around the cab and realize there's another problem here. The truck is a new, huge International. It has no business on a road like this, but then I figure, *Hell, it's not my truck*.

Turns out it's not the driver's truck either, for as soon as we hit deteriorating conditions our friendly driver, whose name is Dave, gets all tense and nervous. Tree branches reach out to scratch the pretty paint job on the sides and smack the $2000 light bar on the cab's roof. Dave says something about how his boss will be agitated by any damage.

Dana replies something about how trucks are meant for abuse.

Then we start downhill.

From the cab the road looks like a brown, knotted rope. I glance over at Dave and see that his fingers have a very good grip on the steering wheel and that his knuckles are beginning to turn pearly white. I reflect on what Dave is going to look like once we get to the bottom of the hill.

Dana and I chat about the idea of living in Montana (more horses and mountains) as if this is just another little ride through the country -- and it is.

Dave seems uninterested in giving his views on the subject. He's pretty engrossed with his driving at this point.

Then we reach the big washout -- or "Dave's Ditch" as I have come to call it.

Dave stops about 20 feet from this hole in the road.

"You guys got around that?" He finally manages to ask (for the life of me, it sounded like his throat was dry.)

"Sure," Dana says. "Just stay close to the bank and you'll be fine."

Of course, I think, *Dave's truck is about 18" wider than Dana's.* I begin to wonder about this myself. Since my window is rolled down, I wonder if I should try to jump clear of the truck if it rolls over the hill or if I should hang on and let the weight of Dana and Dave fall on me and crush me against the door. I am amused by these thoughts rather than threatened, because I am not overly concerned for my safety. I view this whole episode as a great story to tell later on -- if I live.

Still, as we approach the washout, I decide anything would be better than having the truck roll on top of me, so I grasp the handle on the doorjamb.

Dave eases the front wheels around the ditch-to-be, and I wonder if we'll get a cell signal when we're upside-down and 300 feet down in the valley.

As the cab passes the spot, I look down out the window -- I can't see any of the road at this point, just the washout. And on we creep.

Oddly, I can hear Dave holding his breath as he eases the back wheels past the danger. From the look on his face when he glances into his side mirror, I suspect the outside dual tire is over the edge -- 100 yards from the valley floor.

And on we creep.

Finally, Dave gives the all clear when he takes a deep breath.

Dana says, "You know, Matt, I've been thinking about getting a Jeep with a winch on the front. Put a chainsaw and a snatch-block in the back, then we could *really* explore some old roads."

Dave gives Dana a sidelong glance that suggests Dana might be crazy.

Once we reach Dana's truck, Dave hops out like his seat has caught fire. Then, walking around on unsteady legs, he pulls out a cigarette and lighter. This turns out to be a problem since he can't seem to line the cigarette up with the lighter in his shaky hands.

It was fortunate that Dana and I had gotten stuck at place where the road is wide -- well, wider. I doubt that we could have talked Dave into backing all the way down here.

After he finishes his smoke, Dave climbs back into the International and, after pulling forward and backing up about 8 times, he gets turned around and finally has the bed of the rollback close to the rear of Dana's truck.

And I do have to hand it to Dave. By manipulating the hydraulic bed with a cable attached to the frame of Dana's truck via a pulley, Dave gently eases the pick-up out of the new ravine and pulls it onto the firm road.

As he puts the pulley away and gets the bed back in place, Dave looks at me and says, "Ya know, I ain't even a tow truck driver. I'm a mechanic." I look at him and realize he really has gone through hell today, and I offer this compensation, "Yeah, but just think about what a great story you'll get to tell your grandkids someday."

Dave gives me the same are-you-nuts look he gave Dana earlier.

So, when I sign the papers, I do something I'd never done before. I tip him for the tow. $20.

That was compensation he appreciated.

Dana does the same, though I'm not sure how much.

With that, Dave gets back into the truck and begins making tracks. He seems to be in a big hurry to get away from this place.

Dana and I follow, but we soon lose sight of him.

Of course, we all still had to navigate around the washout halfway up the road.

When Dana and I get there, Dave has already gone through, but he has stopped and is walking back. I can see why. Dave's Ditch is now quite a bit wider. In fact, he barely made it through.

Dana stops the truck, and we get out to size things up.

"I felt it give way as I went through," Dave says breathlessly. "I think the bed hit the ground, but I floored it as I came through and made it. I'm not sure you guys can." But instead of looking at the ditch, Dana looks around in the road. After a moment, he points to a place with the toe of his boot.

"Yep," Dana says. "The corner of your bed hit right here."

I look down at the spot, and there it is, an

impression in the soil with a 90-degree angle in it. Since the bed of the truck is about 3 feet off the ground, there was no doubt but what the International's rear wheels had gone into the ravine, into Dave's Ditch, taking several inches of the road with it.

And I realize this is how you learn to track. You always, *always,* observe the world around you and keep on learning. The next time I see an indentation like this on a dirt road, I'll know that a big truck with a rollback bed had nearly disappeared over the mountainside.

Dana, meanwhile, sizes up the road and ditch and confidently announces he'll be able to get through.

I confidently stride over to the other side of the growing ditch to watch him do it.

Dana manages to get the front tires past Dave's Ditch with no problem. But the washout begins to give way under Dana's rear wheels, so he guns the engine and flies over the loose soil. There's bump and a thump, and the roar of the engine, and more of the road caves in.

At first I don't think he'll make it, but he does, and I feel a strong breeze as the truck blows by me.

Dave and I walk back to the ditch across the road. No one's going to be driving a truck down this road for a very long time.

It's a horse trail now.

An hour later, Dana and I are celebrating our adventure over a meal at Shoney's.

"You know, Matt," he says with a gleam in his eyes, "That was the best day I've had in a long time.

"Me too, Dana," I reply. "Me too."

But it is all over too soon.

My thumb is twitching. My hand is shaking, and I have no desire to return to "civilization."

But, I think, *at least I have had one more day in the mountains.*

After Dana and I part ways, instead of heading for the nearest interstate on-ramp, I head back to the mountain. I am in the little red Jeep, the Jeep that whispered its name to me one night: Shiloh.

Halfway there I stop at a little produce stand Curtis used to enjoy visiting from time-to-time. I pick up a can of Pepsi, a candy bar, and an apple for the return trip. I head for the checkout, a wooden bench with an old electric adding machine. I ask the man there for a couple other things. He puts it all in a "poke" -- a small paper bag.

When I reach the top of the mountain, my mind races with thoughts of freedom and horses and Great Granny Akers and my uncertain future.

My cousin Buck recently sent me a photo he found of Great Granny Akers riding a horse. She is elegantly dressed and the horse is well outfitted. No wonder she frowned at the thought of her great grandson carrying a briefcase.

I pass Granny and Curtis' old house as slowly as I dare without attracting attention. I eye the mountain peak above it. For a moment I am envious that my grandparents got to live so much of their lives here. But I also realize that they made that choice, and living a simple life is not to be confused with living an easy life. It's my fault that I wasn't as wise as them. It is time for me to rethink my choices, even as the options close in around me.

I pull on up the road with a bad taste in my mouth. When we drove past here this morning, Dana gave me the bad news: The state has started work to replace this little mountain road with a scenic highway.

Civilization is coming to Akers Mountain.

I drive past the property Cousin Buck owns, property I have thought of trying to buy.

But The State of West Virginia sent him a letter asking for permission to survey his land in the preparation for the "Shawnee Scenic Highway."

He said, "No."

They then sent him a letter saying they would do it anyway.

And they are. Wooden stakes and orange flagging outline the current road right of way. Where I am now driving will someday be a two-lane, paved road with a speed limit of 45-55 mph. People will breeze through here and see this beautiful place through the windows of their cars -- except for the kids, who'll be watching the DVD player. It'll be another paved road where animals will get run over on a regular basis. The litter will pile up. Will there be a travel plaza with an Exxon and Kentucky Fried Chicken at the site of my great grandparents' home and store?

Granny and Curtis' house may be razed to make room for the road. Some of the mountain peak beside it, a place where I have had transcendental experiences, a place that is most sacred, will have to be blasted away to make room for progress.

I'm sure there will be scenic pull-offs, small parking lots. The old song "They paved paradise and put up a parking lot," runs through my head. The pull-offs will have trashcans that overflow and attract the black bears from their natural habitats and ways of life. The scenic highway may be as long as 70 miles. Will there be restrooms and vending machines?

Dana says that several wealthy folks have bought up large tracts of land and this new road will serve their interests most of all. I seriously doubt they will be moving here for the simple life. $150,000 weekend retreats with huge TVs and every creature comfort imaginable will become the norm here.

And there is nothing I can do to stop it.

I cut around to another road and drive just below the ridge for a while. Here the ruts are so deep that even in Jeep Shiloh, I'm afraid I might drag. A car could not make this road.

I come to a little clearing and stop in the middle of the road. I doubt I will block any traffic.

I reach into the poke and pull out a small, foil pouch. Then I climb out of Jeep Shiloh and walk over to a spot in the clearing where Dana first brought me a few years ago.

Here, near my feet, are the bones of three Cherokee Indians. They are not direct ancestors, but they are family all the same. Yes, I have done the genealogy to confirm it, found records and references to my ancestors in history books. As best as I can piece it together, they came to what was then western Virginia to avoid the Trail of Tears, the Removal of southeastern Indian tribes to Oklahoma. They fled here to maintain their freedom, and standing at this spot now, I wonder where I can flee to for the same freedom, the same peace of mind.

There are no stones to mark the graves, and as far as I know, only three other people even know of their existence. I am the youngest.

I feel a certain responsibility.

The small, foil bag in my hand is full of pipe tobacco -- the same brand Curtis used to smoke. I open it gently, dip in and pull out a pinch of the dark and moist leaves. The aroma is beautiful and takes me back to my youth.

I sprinkle the tobacco over the graves. Then I sprinkle it to the east, the south, the west, and finally the north. I say a few words in the form of a prayer. The words are in Cherokee. I've been doing a little homework.

When I finish, I look to the golden red leaves of the trees around me. I feel unusually calm -- the world is nowhere near me.

Time has stopped. My hand is steady.

No, I cannot live the life my grandparents and ancestors did. And with the plans for a new highway, I can't even try. Not here at least. Not anywhere really.

I climb back into the Jeep and sit with my left foot still on the ground. The sun is setting itself down behind a distant ridge. A cool breeze is coming up from the valley. For a moment I feel connected to everything around me, from the rocks to the clouds.

Finally, I draw in my left foot, push in on the clutch, and start the engine.

I have choices to make.

Do I become a mountain hermit?   Do I buy a farm, a horse, and a dog? Do I look for a good woman?

I can reasonably expect to live another 20-30 years. Do I just live my life as it is?

I place my steady right hand on the gear stick.

Do I put it in reverse and go back the way I came?

Or do I go forward?

About a mile ahead there is a fork in the road. If I go forward, should I go left to a little town I know? Or should I go right, not knowing where I might wind up?

I close my eyes, say a little prayer for myself, and make my choice.

I put Jeep Shiloh in gear and slowly let out

the clutch.

In the back of my mind, I hear Curtis' voice as clear as if he were right here in the seat beside me. He is teasing me. "Matthew, I think we're lost," he says.

But I know better.

AFTERWORD

In the seven years since Dana and I were happily stuck on the mountain, many things have changed, few of them for the good.

My parents have both passed away: Dad (*Cash* Clark Wolfe) in May 2011 and Mom in September 2012. The grief has been nearly fatal for me as well. As they wished, I mixed my parents' ashes together and placed a portion of those in two different places on the mountain while Dana looked on. In doing so, I held their ground-up bones in my hand, a loving and comforting act.

This means that of the major "characters" in this memoir, Dana and I are all who remain. Indeed, Dana's wife, Gaye, passed away in 2014. We are now two men stumbling around in our empty houses.

The tremors I describe in my thumb and hand continued to worsen until I was indeed diagnosed with Parkinson's Disease in 2011. It is a life sentence that I am now appealing to a higher authority.

The good news is that Katie did come to visit Mom, her grandmother, shortly before Mom died. Since then, Katie and I see each other from time-to-time and sometimes text a message or two. It's a start.

As for the scenic highway that will change all that is sacred about the mountain, West Virginia's economic troubles have apparently shelved those plans for now.

Finally, I want to tell one last story that fits this collection in a neat way. The day after the trip described in Chapter Six, Jeep Shiloh's transmission sounded like a tornado ripping through an Italian kitchen: large, steel mixing bowls and utensils crashing all over the freaking place. After some investigation, I figured out that when I had had the transmission fluid changed a few months before, the national chain shop that did the work used automatic instead of manual transmission fluid. Shiloh's transmission was scorched and torched. Worse still, no one in town seemed interested in working on it. Several phone calls abruptly ended with the words, "Sorry, we don't have a certified technician for that." I even got that answer from a Jeep dealership. I didn't want a certified technician. I wanted a mechanic worthy of the name.

Technically, the Jeep was nearly totaled – the cost of replacing the transmission would be close to Shiloh's Blue Book "value," probably more. But there is more to value than a price tag.

Finally I heard about this one place through a couple of friends, a place I hadn't heard of before, but I was desperate. I loved the darned thing and hated to give a sturdy piece of machinery up to consumer mentality that easily. I gave the place a call, and without hesitation they said bring it on in.

I called for a rollback to carry Shiloh to salvation.

I immediately liked the garage, Pin Point Auto, a family owned garage with mechanics who knew their stuff. I spied everything going on at once: from oil changes to racecar building. It reminded me of the garages Curtis worked in when I was a kid.

It took a few days to locate a rebuilt transmission (it was shipped from a Jeep "graveyard" in Michigan), but they did it. And they installed it. At 3 AM on a Saturday morning. And they did it well.

Shiloh and I have covered over 60,000 miles since that early morning transmission transplant with trips to Key West, Florida; Halifax, Nova Scotia; and Fairbanks, Alaska via the famous Alaska Highway (Those books are in the pipeline on the same computer I am using to type up this afterword).

The lesson? Just as I allude to throughout this book: avoid the corporate chain stores when you can. Shop local. Find the family businesses. Learn their names.   Wave to them as you pass each other at the local bank.

-- Matthew Wolfe, Fall 2017

www.ingramcontent.com/pod-product-compliance
Lightning Source LLC
Chambersburg PA
CBHW061729020426
42331CB00006B/1169